What in the World is God Doing?

ROBERT GRIFFITH

GRACE AND TRUTH PUBLISHING
P.O. Box 338, Gunnedah NSW 2380 Australia
www.graceandtruthpublishing.com.au

ISBN 978-1-7642635-5-9

TABLE OF CONTENTS

INTRODUCTION

"What in the world is God doing?" For many today, this phrase is not a question at all but an exclamation - spoken in frustration, confusion, or even fear. In a world which is now marked by wars, political upheaval, moral uncertainty, economic instability, and cultural turbulence, many look around and wonder whether God has withdrawn from human history altogether.

Even many Christians quietly ask themselves if the days of great spiritual movements are over, if revival is now a relic of some bygone era, remembered fondly but no longer experienced.

But the very same words - *what in the world is God doing?* - can be understood another way: not as a cry of despair, but as a genuine question of faith, expectation, and curiosity. Because despite the shadows that seem to engulf so much of the modern world, God is certainly not absent, silent, or inactive.

Quite the opposite is in fact the case. Across continents, cultures, and denominations, the Spirit of God is moving in ways both dramatic and subtle, both public and hidden, both historic and quietly unfolding. Revival is not a memory; it is a present reality. This book is a sincere attempt to answer that very question - not exhaustively, for no single volume could contain all that God is doing in the world - but meaningfully.

Each chapter highlights a movement of God in a particular place or through a particular stream of renewal: awakenings in Latin America; the powerful house-church growth across China; supernatural dreams among Muslims; historic outpourings in Toronto, Brownsville, and Smithton; global prayer movements; the Alpha Course renewal; the persistence of revival in Africa; Korean mountains alive with intercession; and the surprising return of spiritual hunger in the secular West.

These stories span nations, cultures, and traditions, yet they share a common thread: God is at work in our generation, often in places and ways we least expect.

This is not a book of nostalgia. It is not a sentimental tour of the past. It is a factual, global, contemporary exploration of revival and spiritual renewal – rooted in verifiable reports, historical evidence, and the testimonies of countless believers and leaders worldwide. This book will show that the Kingdom of God is still advancing, that the gospel is spreading, and that the church is growing even in the midst of all the political oppression, cultural resistance, and religious hostility.

This is also a book of encouragement. Many believers today feel overwhelmed by the darkness they see around them. But when we lift our eyes beyond our immediate circumstances - when we look to Iran's underground church; the worship movements in Africa; Asia's revival fires; and Europe's surprising return to prayer - we will rediscover the truth that Jesus announced over two thousand years ago: *"My Father is always at his work to this very day."* (John 5:17).

What in the world is God doing? Far more than we can imagine and the pages which now follow are my imperfect, incomplete, yet sincere attempt to offer you a window into His ongoing story of redemption in our world.

1. THE ASHBURY OUTPOURING (2023)
A GENERATION AWAKENS

On the morning of Wednesday, 8 February 2023, a small group of students at Asbury University gathered for their usual mid-week chapel service - one of the hundreds of routine gatherings that had taken place on that campus for more than a century. Nothing on the schedule hinted that anything unusual was about to occur. The speaker, a local pastor, delivered a straightforward message from Romans 12 about sincere love, transforming grace, and living as a sacrificial community shaped by God's mercy. When the service ended, students were free to leave for class or lunch, just as they always did.

However, about twenty students stayed behind. They lingered in prayer and worship, unhurried and unpressured. That simple decision - to remain when everyone else left - became the spark of something extraordinary.

Over the next hour or so, more students drifted back into Hughes Auditorium. A handful soon became dozens, and dozens then became hundreds. Word quietly spread across campus: *"God is here."* Many who had left chapel earlier sensed a pull to return.

By mid-afternoon, the whole auditorium was full. Worship rose spontaneously - no worship team, no production, no lights, no screens. Students read Scripture aloud, confessed their sins, prayed for one another, and sang songs from memory or from a simple guitar. Many later described the atmosphere using words such as *"peace," "holy love," "joy," "gentleness,"* and *"the nearness of Jesus."* As one student put it, *"It felt like God had walked into the room and sat among us ... and He did not leave."*

What began as an ordinary chapel service soon expanded into a 16-day, round-the-clock, unbroken gathering of worship, prayer, repentance, and testimony. The doors of Hughes Auditorium remained open day and night as thousands of people streamed in from across the United States and eventually from nations around the world.

The university - normally a quiet Christian campus in Wilmore, Kentucky, became the destination of a global pilgrimage. Social media spread the news across the world within hours. Major news outlets arrived shortly after. Lines formed outside the chapel and stretched around the block, sometimes for hours, as people waited to enter the building where God seemed to be drawing near with unusual tenderness.

The small town of Wilmore, population just over 6,000, was overwhelmed. Restaurants ran out of food. Parking overflowed into neighbouring towns. Local authorities eventually had to redirect traffic and limit access, because so many visitors were arriving each day. Estimates suggest that more than 50,000 people came through Wilmore during this outpouring - an astonishing reality for a quiet college town. The world noticed. But more importantly, the church noticed.

Throughout Scripture, God often chose small, unlikely places as the birthplace of renewal. In 1 Samuel 16:11, we read where Samuel was seeking Israel's next king, and he overlooked the seven impressive sons of Jesse until God directed him to David, the shepherd boy in the field. When Jesus began His ministry, He chose fishermen, a tax collector, and a zealot rather than trained religious elites (Matthew 4:18–22).

When the Holy Spirit was poured out at Pentecost, it happened among an unimpressive group of disciples waiting in obedience in an upper room (Acts 2:1–4). God regularly starts big things in small places. Asbury 2023 followed that very familiar divine pattern - a small town, a modest chapel, and a generation often labelled spiritually indifferent, became the unexpected epicentre of a fresh move of God.

A move of God without a stage

One of the most striking features of the Asbury Outpouring was its simplicity. There was no famous preacher. No celebrity worship leader. No production crew. No conference schedule. No brand. No marketing.

The university leadership team deliberately refused to platform personalities; instead, they allowed students to lead almost everything. They read Scripture, initiated prayer times, shared testimonies, and led worship using a single acoustic guitar or piano. There was no attempt to orchestrate the moment. There was simply an openness to the Spirit of God.

Humility marked the atmosphere. A quiet reverence seemed to fill the room. People described a tangible sense of God's holiness, leading many into repentance. Others were drawn to deep intercession. Some knelt at the altar for hours; others sat silently in their seats, overwhelmed by the presence of God. There was unity - a spiritual harmony impossible to manufacture. As the psalmist writes, *"The Lord is close to the broken-hearted and saves those who are crushed in spirit."* (Psalm 34:18). That closeness became the hallmark of those days.

The simplicity of the gathering became a theological statement: when God moves, God Himself becomes the focus. Worship becomes less about performance and more about surrender; less about creating an atmosphere and more about recognising His presence. The absence of spectacle revealed the essence of revival - Jesus was at the centre, His people were humbled and hungry before Him.

The hunger of a generation

Much has been written about Gen Z, often with a pessimistic tone. Analysts describe them as digitally distracted, emotionally fragile, socially disconnected, and increasingly secular. But beneath the surface lies a deep spiritual hunger - a longing for authenticity, meaning, community, and truth. This generation has grown weary of performance religion, political polarisation, and shallow spirituality. They want something real.

Asbury 2023 offered what their souls were starving for: the unhurried presence of God. Students testified to being freed from anxiety, depression, and shame. Others spoke of restored relationships, renewed faith, or first-time encounters with Christ.

Some who had grown up in church but drifted away, returned with fresh conviction. The fruit was not loud or dramatic but deep, gentle, and genuine.

One student wrote, *"For the first time in my life, I feel free."* Another said, *"I have known Jesus for years, but I have never felt His love like this."* A faculty member noted, *"These students are encountering the holiness of God, and it is transforming them."*

Testimonies like these spread quickly around the world, fuelling renewed anticipation for a move of God among young people who had been largely written off as spiritually disengaged. What happened at Asbury was revival from the inside out.

A spark that leapt across campuses

In a matter of days, other universities began to experience similar gatherings - Lee University in Tennessee, Samford University in Alabama, Cedarville University in Ohio, Baylor University in Texas, and more. So many students spontaneously filled chapels, classrooms, and prayer rooms with unplanned worship and prayer. These campuses were not copying Asbury. They simply sought God, and God met them.

This is a consistent biblical pattern: revival is not a product but a flame. It cannot be franchised. It spreads where hearts are open. Jesus described the movement of the Holy Spirit like the wind - unpredictable, uncontrollable, sovereign (John 3:8).

This Asbury Outpouring became a kind of spiritual weather system, and campuses across America found themselves caught in its currents.

The timing was remarkable. After years of global disruption - pandemic anxiety, political division, social fragmentation, and widespread cultural confusion - God initiated a fresh move among the generation most deeply affected by these pressures. It was as if He was saying, *"I have not abandoned this generation. I am calling them to Myself."*

A humble beginning to a larger story

What happened at Asbury in 2023 was not merely an isolated event. It was a signpost - a quiet, yet powerful reminder that God is still at work in the world. A small, unassuming chapel in rural Kentucky became the birthplace of a renewed hunger for prayer, holiness, and the presence of God. It inspired believers across continents, encouraged exhausted pastors, awakened spiritual curiosity among so many secular observers, and catalysed fresh movements of worship and repentance.

The story of Asbury is still unfolding, and its impact continues to ripple outward. God began something in those days that would echo across many churches, universities, and nations - a testimony that He is not done with His people, and He is not done with this generation.

The anatomy of a modern outpouring

To understand the significance of the Asbury Outpouring, it is important to move beyond the headlines and examine the deeper movements of the Spirit that defined those sixteen days. Revival is not merely a large gathering of Christians, nor is it simply an emotional moment which is heightened by music or atmosphere. Genuine revival is always a sovereign work of God marked by repentance, holiness, reconciliation, transformed lives, and an intensified awareness of His presence. At Asbury, these marks were consistently evident.

One of the earliest and most repeated themes was confession. Students stood and openly acknowledged hidden sins, long-held bitterness, secret addictions, and brokenness they had kept buried. They did so without coercion, without pressure, and without fear of judgment. Instead, there was a collective sense that the holiness of God made honesty safe.

When revival comes, light exposes darkness - but without any condemnation. Many students said they felt a strong but gentle conviction, a drawing back to the heart of God Himself, and an overwhelming assurance of His love even as they confessed their failures.

This dynamic is deeply biblical. When Isaiah encountered the presence of God, he cried out, *"Woe to me! ...I am a man of unclean lips."* (Isaiah 6:5). When Peter confronted the power of Jesus, he fell at His knees and said, *"Go away from me, Lord; I am a sinful man!"* (Luke 5:8).

The holiness of God will never crush the repentant heart; it will always restore it. At Asbury, confession was also followed by forgiveness, reconciliation, and healing. Students prayed for one another, embraced one another, and often wept together as God mended relationships and renewed hope.

Alongside confession came worship: simple, unpolished, deeply sincere worship. The songs were often initiated spontaneously, either by a student on the platform or from someone just in the congregation. There were no predetermined setlists. Some lyrics written on paper or displayed on a phone screen were enough.

Many commented that they had never experienced worship with so little production yet so much power. The freedom of the Spirit was evident not in noise or spectacle but in the unity, humility, and authenticity of the voices raised in praise.

The worship reflected a longing for God Himself, not for an experience. It was not driven by emotional manipulation, dramatic crescendos, or charismatic personalities. Instead, a holy hunger permeated the room - a desire for Jesus, for His presence, for His truth, for His nearness. This was the heartbeat of revival.

The theological significance of what God did

The Asbury Outpouring raised important theological questions. Was this truly a revival? What constitutes revival in a biblical sense? How should the church interpret what happened? These questions deserve careful reflection.

Scripture presents revival not as a one-time event but as a recurring pattern in the life of God's people. Throughout the Old Testament, God repeatedly called Israel to repentance, renewal, and return. When the people responded with humility, God restored them and poured out His blessing.

The same pattern appears in the New Testament as believers continually seek the filling and empowering of the Holy Spirit (Acts 4:31; Ephesians 5:18). Revival, therefore, is not a novelty, it is a normal part of the ongoing life of God's people, sparked by His grace and sustained by His Spirit.

What happened at Asbury aligns with all these biblical themes. There was repentance, prayer, humility, worship, unity, and a renewed commitment to holiness. The fruit was consistent with the character of God Himself. Students were drawn not toward emotionalism but toward Scripture, prayer, and discipleship. Many reported that their desire for sin diminished while their desire for Christ intensified. Such outcomes reflect the Spirit's work, not human enthusiasm.

Another significant aspect of Asbury was its restraint. Leaders refused to sensationalise this special moment. They guarded the gathering from becoming a spectacle. They resisted attempts to turn it into a platform for well-known preachers or worship leaders. This decision prevented the outpouring from being hijacked by personalities or agendas. In many ways, their restraint protected the authenticity of what God was doing.

This restraint also aligned with a critical biblical principle: God moves most powerfully when human pride is humbled. The Lord said to Isaiah, *"I live...with the one who is contrite and lowly in spirit."* (Isaiah 57:15). At Asbury, there were no egos in the spotlight. The posture of the leaders allowed God to remain at the centre.

Global resonance and worldwide attention

What happened in that small auditorium was not contained to Wilmore. The world was watching - not out of curiosity alone, but out of longing. Believers across nations felt a quiet ache in their spirits, a yearning for God to do something similar in their own context. churches and youth groups livestreamed the outpouring. Pastors travelled long distances simply to sit in the atmosphere of worship and return home with renewed hope.

Missionaries in remote places reported that just hearing about Asbury strengthened their faith. Even secular commentators took note, surprised by the sheer size, sincerity, and staying power of the gathering.

One significant reason for the outpouring's global impact was its timing. The world in 2023 was still wrestling with the emotional and spiritual aftermath of the COVID-19 pandemic. Fear, grief, social division, and mental health crises were widespread. Many young people were struggling under the weight of anxiety, uncertainty, and the loss of community. In such a landscape, God's gentle move at Asbury felt like a divine intervention. It was a reminder that He sees, He cares, and He is near.

This moment also resonated globally because it contradicted the dominant narrative of secular decline. For decades, analysts have predicted the collapse of Christian faith in the Western world. Yet in a time when many declared that God was no longer at work among the next generation, He moved in a way that was impossible to ignore. Revival broke out not in a megachurch, not on a conference stage, not through celebrity influence, but in a humble university chapel filled with ordinary students.

This was a theological statement in itself: God is not bound by cultural trends. He is not intimidated by secularism. He is not limited by the doubts of a generation. The outpouring reminded the church that God is sovereign in His timing and His methods. As Jesus said, *"My Father is always at his work to this very day."* (John 5:17).

The ripple effect across churches

churches across America and beyond reported a renewed hunger for prayer following the Asbury Outpouring. Weekly prayer meetings increased in attendance. Pastors found their congregations were more responsive to worship, repentance, and discipleship. Many believers felt stirred to seek God more intentionally, to fast, to pray, and to confess hidden sin. This was not enthusiasm stirred by hype. It was conviction stirred by holiness.

In some places, church leaders intentionally avoided trying to "recreate Asbury." Instead, they sought to cultivate a posture of openness to God's presence in their own community. They recognised that revival is not a lightning strike but a spiritual climate change. God begins with repentance, humility, and hunger, and the effects ripple outward over weeks, months, and even years.

Testimonies emerged of individuals who travelled to Wilmore and returned home transformed. Some experienced a renewed call to ministry. Others were stirred to evangelism. Many re-entered their local churches with a fresh fire for prayer. Youth pastors reported that their students - who had watched or visited - became more engaged and spiritually awakened.

These ripples demonstrate a very important truth: the Asbury Outpouring was not the finish line. It was a beginning, a spark, a sign that God is still drawing near to His people.

A generation marked by holiness and hope

Perhaps the most important legacy of the Asbury Outpouring will be the imprint it left on a generation. Many of the students involved were at a formative stage of life—making decisions about identity, faith, future, and purpose. To encounter God so deeply at that age is profoundly shaping.

Some will carry the memory of those days for decades. Many will become pastors, missionaries, worship leaders, teachers, counsellors, and parents who lead future generations into the presence of God.

The outpouring also challenged the wider church to reconsider how it views young people. Rather than writing them off as apathetic or unreachable, Asbury revealed that when Jesus is lifted high, young hearts respond with surprising passion and sincerity. The hunger for God is not dead. It has simply been buried under layers of distraction and noise. But when the Spirit moves, those layers fall away and something beautiful emerges.

Why revival matters in the twenty-first century

To appreciate the significance of the Asbury Outpouring, it must be understood within the broader spiritual landscape of our time. Western culture has undergone rapid secularisation. Many young adults no longer identify with any religion. churches have struggled to retain emerging generations. Digital saturation has fragmented attention. Mental health struggles have become widespread. Cynicism, loneliness, and existential uncertainty shape much of contemporary life.

Against this backdrop, revival is not merely an interesting spiritual event—it is a prophetic announcement. It testifies that God is not withdrawing from the world. He is not retreating from university campuses. He has not abandoned the next generation. Instead, He is moving directly into the places where faith appears to be fading, reigniting a hunger for His presence.

Revival is a reminder that the church is not sustained by human strategy, cultural power, or technological innovation. It is sustained by the Spirit of God. When the Holy Spirit moves, He realigns priorities, softens hearts, awakens spiritual hunger, and reorders affections. He reveals Jesus with clarity and beauty. He confronts sin not to condemn but to heal. Revival is God doing what only God can do.

At Asbury, revival mattered because it offered hope. Hope to exhausted pastors who had laboured through years of division and discouragement. Hope to parents praying for wayward children. Hope to students who had never experienced a genuine move of God. Hope to Christians who feared the future of faith in their culture. Revival reminded them that God is still writing the story.

Balancing experience with discernment

As with all movements of God, Asbury also invited discernment. Revival is never a flawless or perfectly tidy phenomenon. Whenever the Holy Spirit moves, human weakness is present alongside divine power.

The New Testament church, even under apostolic leadership, was often messy - full of questions, misunderstandings, excesses, and tensions. Yet God worked powerfully through that imperfect community to birth the global church.

In the same way, the Asbury Outpouring required spiritual maturity. Leaders at the university continually emphasised the need for humility, order, and biblical grounding. Scriptural reading was central. Students were encouraged to test absolutely everything by the Word of God. Emotional displays were neither promoted nor discouraged; the focus remained on Christ.

Times of silence were as common as times of singing. The leadership made sure that the room did not become a place of spectacle but a place of sacred encounter.

Every revival throughout history has required this balance. In Thessalonica, Paul urged believers not to *"quench the Spirit,"* yet also to *"test them all."* (1 Thessalonians 5:19–21). At Asbury, both instructions were carefully honoured. The Spirit was welcomed wholeheartedly, but the movement was anchored in Scripture, prayer, and wise oversight.

This balance helped protect the outpouring from error, distraction, or emotional manipulation. It also strengthened the credibility of the movement in the eyes of observers - both believers and sceptics. Revival is not validated by popularity but by fruit, and Asbury's fruit was evident: repentance, reconciliation, renewed devotion, and transformed lives.

A new model for revival in a digital age

Another unique characteristic of the Asbury Outpouring was its relationship to technology. Social media played a significant role in the spread of news. Students posted short clips of worship or testimonies online, and within hours millions of people around the world were aware that something unusual was happening. People who lived thousands of kilometres away could see glimpses of the gathering on their phones.

Yet interestingly, the outpouring itself remained intentionally low-tech. Screens were minimal. Production was non-existent. Leaders discouraged filming during worship, encouraging people instead to be fully present to God. Visitors often reported that the contrast between the digital world and the sacred stillness of the chapel was striking. Many said they had not experienced that kind of quiet reverence in years. The combination of rapid digital communication and simple spiritual depth created a distinctly twenty-first-century revival dynamic.

In previous generations, news of revival spread through newspapers, letters, and word of mouth. Today, it spreads through short videos and online testimonies. Yet the core reality remains the same: God awakens hunger, and people respond. Technology may amplify awareness, but the Spirit of God ignites the flame.

Asbury's low-tech, presence-centred approach became a subtle critique of modern Christianity's growing tendency toward entertainment and spectacle. It reminded the church that revival does not require perfect aesthetics, creative programming, or charismatic personalities. It requires hearts that are wide open, humble, and desperate for God.

The witness of a watching world

One of the most unexpected aspects of the Asbury Outpouring was the attention it received from secular observers. Journalists, commentators, and influencers who did not share the Christian faith nevertheless expressed curiosity and even admiration for what they saw. Many noted the sincerity, the simplicity, and the absence of celebrity. Others remarked on the emotional health of the students or the peaceful atmosphere of the gatherings.

This public witness is very important. Revival, when genuine, displays the character of God in a way that even sceptics can recognise. While belief may not immediately follow, respect often does. Revival shows that Christianity is not merely a cultural institution, but a living movement shaped by the presence of the risen Christ.

It reminds the world that faith is not a private hobby but a vibrant, communal encounter with the living God. The Asbury Outpouring offered a counter-narrative to the fractured and polarised world of 2023. In a time dominated by political hostility, online outrage, and cultural tension, Asbury became a space of peace, confession, forgiveness, and reconciliation.

Young people of different backgrounds worshipped together, prayed together, and embraced one another as brothers and sisters in Christ. In a world defined by division, such unity itself was a testimony to the power of the gospel.

Jesus said, *"By this everyone will know that you are my disciples, if you love one another."* (John 13:35). That love was on display in a very public way, and people noticed.

Long-term fruit and ongoing stories

Revival cannot be measured only by what happens during the event itself. It's true impact is seen in the months and years that follow. For many, the Asbury Outpouring became a real spiritual turning point. Students who encountered God in those days returned to classrooms, families, churches, and communities carrying a renewed devotion to Jesus Christ. Many testified to lasting transformation: addictions broken, identities clarified, relationships restored, and vocational callings affirmed.

Some people reported that anxiety and depression - long-term struggles - lifted in the presence of God. Others found boldness in sharing the gospel with friends or co-workers. Several sensed a call to ministry or mission. Many simply experienced a rekindled love for Jesus that reshaped their daily lives.

churches and ministries connected to students involved in the outpouring also reported ongoing fruit. Prayer meetings that had been sparsely attended before became vibrant. Bible studies multiplied. Worship gatherings deepened significantly. A subtle but noticeable shift took place in many communities: a renewed expectation that God would move.

This expectation is itself a form of revival. When believers anticipate the presence of God, they pray differently, worship differently, think differently, and live differently. Revival becomes not an event but a posture - a way of seeing the world and a way of walking with God.

The broader significance for the global church

The Asbury Outpouring functioned as a sign, and a signal from heaven that God is stirring His people across the world. It was not an isolated flare, but part of a larger constellation of spiritual activity that has been building globally: explosive growth in the Iranian church, extraordinary reports of dreams and visions among Muslims, unprecedented evangelistic harvests in parts of Africa and Latin America, and deep hunger for prayer in many nations.

Asbury reminds the church that revival is not confined to specific cultures or generations. God is at work everywhere - often quietly, often unexpectedly, often in places where spiritual hunger is hidden beneath cultural noise. The Spirit moves across boundaries of ethnicity, language, geography, and tradition. His work is global, diverse, and unstoppable.

In this sense, Asbury serves as a doorway into the broader story this book will explore. What God did in that small Kentucky chapel is connected to what He is doing in the underground churches in Iran, on prayer mountains in South Korea, in youth movements in Brazil, and in campus ministries across the West. Revival is not a random spark - it is part of a divine tapestry.

A sign of hope for a weary world

At its core, the Asbury Outpouring revealed one profound truth: God delights to draw near to His people. When hearts are humble, when worship is sincere, and when hunger for His presence rises, He comes. Not because we earn His presence, but because He is gracious and loves to reveal Himself. The world in 2023 was weary. Students were weary. churches were weary. Pastors were weary.

Into that weariness, God breathed fresh life. He reminded His people that He is still Emmanuel - God with us. He is still the Good Shepherd who restores souls. He is still the One who sends rivers into dry places and gives beauty for ashes.

Revival is not the end of the story. It is the beginning of renewal. And the Asbury Outpouring stands as a living testimony that, even in a secular age, God is moving - quietly, powerfully, unexpectedly - awakening a generation to the beauty of Jesus.

2. IRAN'S UNDERGROUND AWAKENING
THE FASTEST GROWING CHURCH IN THE WORLD

In the Islamic Republic of Iran, a remarkable and largely hidden movement of faith has been quietly unfolding. Behind the fences of fear, beneath the radar of the regime, and in the privacy of homes and apartments, thousands of Iranians are discovering the gospel of Jesus Christ and meeting in house church gatherings.

For years, Christian observers spoke about the "underground church" in Iran; recently secular research, asylum-cases, and human rights reports have affirmed that the hidden Christian presence may number in the hundreds of thousands or more.

This story begins with the context of the Iranian revolution of 1979, which turned Iran into a theocratic Shiite state under the clerical leadership of the Ayatollahs. Islam became not only a religion but a political identity; apostasy, proselytising from Islam, or conversion to Christianity became dangerous matters. Yet out of this context of control and suppression emerged a church that would grow when most expected decline. One researcher recently said Iran is now *"witnessing the highest rate of Christianization in the world."*

The shift from public to private faith

In earlier decades, the Christian presence in Iran was primarily confined to the ethnic Armenian and Assyrian minorities, whose churches enjoyed legal recognition and language-rights. Their communities were historically established, visible, and relatively protected. But starting in the late 1990s and accelerating after the early 2000s, a whole new phenomenon arose: Persian-speaking Iranians, formerly Muslim, meeting for worship in homes, in small groups, in secret.

These "house churches" usually consisted of 10–15 believers gathering in a private apartment, meeting quietly for worship, Bible study, prayer, and fellowship.

One account describes how the door would lock once all were inside, a guitar would quietly strum, Scripture would be read, communion observed, and then each person would leave individually so as not to attract attention.

This shift mattered for three key reasons:

1. *Language and cultural relevance:* Meeting in Persian, rather than Armenian or Assyrian, meant the gospel reached the majority of Iranians.

2. *Flexibility and mobility:* Without large church buildings or formal structures, small groups could multiply and go underground.

3. *Spiritual hunger:* Many younger Iranians were disillusioned with the official religious system and found in Christ an alternative that spoke to their sense of meaning, identity, and hope.

A growth that defies expectation

Estimating numbers in an underground setting is fraught with difficulty, and nobody pretends these figures are exact. Nevertheless, multiple sources indicate that the Christian movement in Iran is growing rapidly - far faster than the regime anticipates.

In a 2020 survey by the Netherlands-based research group GAMAAN, 1.5% of respondents identified as Christian. When this proportion was extrapolated to Iran's adult population, it implied numbers between several hundred thousand and over one million believers.

Mission organisations provide cautious if larger estimates. One report suggested the number of converts and house-church members may be in the range of one to two million.

A 2017 study conducted by *Landinfo* estimated that many Christian organisations now believe there are "hundreds of thousands" of converts, and that the growth rate of these networks was around 20% per year.

Part of the growth is explained by what one Iranian church-leader called "quiet discipleship" - believers introducing friends to Christ, Bible-reading online, sharing testimonies via satellite TV, and multiplying house-churches in urban centres like Tehran, Isfahan, Karaj, and Rasht.

The cost of faith

Growth has not been without cost. For converts from Islam, declaring allegiance to Christ frequently means loss of family, employment, education, and housing rights. Meeting in homes is illegal when led by converts; distribution of Christian literature in Persian is banned; and the government views unregistered churches as a national security threat.

Since the early 2000s, reports of house-church raids, arrests, long prison sentences, and physical mistreatment have increased. In 2024, for example, one rights organisation reported that the number of Christians sentenced in Iran rose six-fold compared to the previous year.

This is a typical risk scenario: authorities burst into an apartment meeting, confiscate all the phones, Bibles, computers; charge participants under Article 500 of the Penal Code for *"propaganda against Islam"* and membership in *"anti-state"* groups; sentences of eight, ten, or more years follow; sometimes labour-camp detention or family intimidation.

And yet, in the face of persecution, believers display persistent faith. One underground leader shared: *"When we were Muslims, we were ready to die for Allah, who is a distant and cruel God. How much more we are ready to die for Jehovah who is an intimate and loving God."*

A deeper spiritual catalyst

While political, social, and cultural factors contribute to the growth of the Iranian church, the spiritual dimension cannot be ignored. Many converts cite visions, dreams, and supernatural encounters as pivotal to their faith journey - though these are hard to quantify reliably.

Reports from several ministries indicate that Iranian Muslims have experienced dreams of Christ, angels, and spiritual longing which prompted their search for Christian community. We will explore this amazing phenomenon more in the next chapter.

Such testimonies reinforce a theological truth: revival can often happen under the radar, where the presence of God meets people in hidden places, and where seed-planting is quiet but sure. The words of Jesus resonate: *"When the Son of Man comes, will he find faith on the earth?"* (Luke 18:8) In Iran today, many believe He already has.

The power of the Persian testimony

One of the most compelling features of Iran's underground awakening is the central role of personal testimony. In a nation where open evangelism is illegal, the gospel spreads primarily through relationships - family connections, trusted friendships, or workplace conversations. Iranians are renowned for their hospitality, warmth, and deep relational bonds. When someone encounters Christ, the transformation is often profound, unmistakable, and difficult to hide, even if the believer must remain cautious.

Many testimonies share a common theme: a deep dissatisfaction with the religious status quo. For countless Iranians, Islam is not merely a set of spiritual beliefs, it is an omnipresent force shaping politics, law, education, and culture. After decades of theocratic rule, many disillusioned young adults began questioning the ideological narrative they had been raised under. They saw corruption among religious officials, restrictions on personal freedom, and severe consequences for dissent. They felt the weight of mandatory religious observance with no sense of spiritual life underneath. They longed for something authentic, something liberating, something personal.

Into this spiritual vacuum, the message of Jesus has entered like a breath of fresh air. For many, the gospel represents far more than a new religious system; it represents a personal encounter with a God who sees them, loves them, forgives them, and calls them His own.

The contrast between enforced religious duty and the grace of Christ is dramatic. Numerous testimonies describe tears of joy upon reading that Jesus said, *"Come to me, all you who are weary and burdened, and I will give you rest."* (Matthew 11:28). To a people weary of religious oppression, those words strike deeply.

Stories abound of men and women encountering Scripture for the first time. In some cases, people discover online Farsi Bibles or New Testaments downloaded secretly onto their phones. Others find handwritten copies passed quietly among trusted friends. Some gather around satellite television broadcasts by Christian ministries beaming into Iran from abroad. These broadcasts, in Farsi, have become lifelines for many who cannot safely meet with others. They provide preaching, worship, and teaching in the heart language of a people hungry for truth.

As new believers grow in their faith, discipleship becomes a lifeline. House-church leaders typically guide small groups through the Scriptures, often starting with the Gospel of John. Believers learn how to pray, how to read the Bible, how to resist fear, and how to share their faith carefully. This discipleship is crucial, for even the smallest misstep can place the entire group at risk. Yet despite the danger, believers continue to gather. Their testimonies reveal a faith not driven by enthusiasm alone but by a deep, enduring conviction that Jesus is worth everything.

The quiet courage of Iranian women

One of the most surprising features of Iran's revival is the prominent role played by women. In a society where women face legal and cultural restrictions, many Iranian women have become bold evangelists, worship leaders, and discipleship mentors within the underground church. Their courage is remarkable. They are often the first to gather small groups of neighbours or friends, the first to offer hospitality, and the first to nurture spiritual growth in new believers.

This is not merely a demographic observation; it is a theological reality. Many women testify that, in finding Christ, they also discovered dignity and value they had long been denied.

They found a Saviour who spoke with honour to women, who welcomed them as disciples, who revealed Himself first to a woman after His resurrection, and who invited them into the full life of the kingdom of God. In the pages of the New Testament, they found a God who sees them, hears them, and loves them.

It is no surprise, then, that many women report a profound sense of empowerment in their faith. They do not seek power in a worldly sense; rather, they experience spiritual boldness rooted in the love of Jesus. This boldness fuels the growth of the church. Women gather small groups, teach Scripture, lead prayer, and share their testimonies. They serve as the beating heart of many house churches.

This female-led dynamic has drawn attention from researchers and religious freedom advocates. It challenges assumptions about revival and highlights the way God often moves among those whom society overlooks. In Iran, as in the ministry of Jesus, women have become some of the first witnesses of a new work of God.

Miracles in the shadows

Among the most frequently reported elements of Iran's underground awakening are stories of healing, deliverance, and dreams. These testimonies must be handled with care, for not every story is verifiable. However, there is a consistent pattern: a significant number of Iranian converts describe supernatural encounters that led them to seek Christ.

Some speak of visions of Jesus appearing in white, calling them by name. Others describe dreams in which they saw a man with nail-pierced hands inviting them to follow Him. A number report miraculously answered prayers, healings from chronic pain, or deliverance from oppressive fear. While such reports cannot be quantified, they are too widespread to ignore. What is striking is the way many Iranians interpret these experiences. In a culture where dreams have long held spiritual significance, a supernatural encounter often becomes the catalyst for seeking truth.

Many search for explanations online. Some discover Christian sites, satellite broadcasts, or digital Bibles. For these individuals, the supernatural encounter is not the end but the beginning - a step that leads them toward the Scriptures, toward Jesus, and into the fellowship of believers.

This echoes the biblical pattern of God revealing Himself in visions. Throughout Scripture, God used dreams to speak to Pharaoh, Nebuchadnezzar, Joseph, Daniel, and Joseph the earthly father of Jesus. He used visions to confront Saul on the Damascus road, to guide Cornelius, and to encourage Peter. In contexts where access to Scripture is limited and Christian witness is restricted, God often speaks in ways that cannot be blocked by persecution or censorship. Dreams pierce through walls and borders. Visions bypass interrogations and surveillance. The Spirit moves where the Spirit wills.

Digital discipleship in a restricted nation

Iran's underground church has grown not only through personal testimony and supernatural encounters but also through digital evangelism. Technology - ironically controlled by the regime - has become a powerful tool for gospel witness.

Despite the heavy government censorship, millions of Iranians bypass restrictions through VPNs and encrypted applications. These tools allow them to access Christian content, livestream sermons, download Bibles, and connect with believers abroad.

Online discipleship communities allow isolated Christians - especially those in smaller towns - to participate in teaching, prayer, and worship. Leaders from outside the country often mentor Iranian believers through secure video calls, providing theological training and pastoral guidance. This digital lifeline has become essential for the survival of many house-church networks.

Satellite television remains another tool. Christian broadcasters have reported receiving thousands of calls, emails, and messages from Iranians seeking prayer, guidance, or a copy of the Bible.

Satellite signals are not easily blocked, and many Iranians secretly tune in late at night. The gospel message enters homes quietly, invisibly, consistently.

This digital dimension highlights the creativity of the underground church. When one door is closed, another opens. When one method is restricted, another emerges. Far from hindering the gospel, persecution has forced believers to innovate. Every barrier becomes an opportunity for God's wisdom to shine.

The unlikely alliance of suffering and hope

The Iranian revival is marked by an unusual mixture of suffering and hope. Believers gather with the constant knowledge that their meeting may be raided. They share the gospel knowing that a neighbour could report them. They baptise new believers in secret, aware that discovery could mean imprisonment. And yet they do not live in despair. On the contrary, they display a deep joy that many Western Christians find startling.

This joy is not naive happiness. It is a spiritual confidence rooted in the presence of Christ. It echoes the words of the apostles, who rejoiced that they were counted worthy to suffer for His name (Acts 5:41). It mirrors the testimony of Paul, who wrote from prison with unshakeable hope and joy. It reflects the witness of a persecuted church whose faith is purified in the fire.

For Iranian believers, suffering is not an obstacle to revival - it is the soil in which revival grows. Hope rises not in spite of hardship but through it. They see their trials as a participation in the sufferings of Christ, and a testimony to the value of the gospel. This perspective reveals the depth of their discipleship. They do not seek comfort; they seek Christ. And in finding Him, they discover meaning in their suffering.

Their hope is sustained by the wonderful promises of Scripture: *"We are hard pressed on every side, but not crushed... persecuted, but not abandoned."* (2 Corinthians 4:8–9). *"Those who sow with tears will reap with songs of joy."* (Psalm 126:5).

These verses are not theoretical to them; they are daily realities. The Iranian church lives in the tension of pain and joy, persecution and revival, risk and reward—and through it all, Christ is glorified.

Discipleship in the dark: church growth without buildings

One of the most astonishing aspects of Iran's underground awakening is that it has grown without the typical structures that Western Christians take for granted. There are no church buildings for Persian-speaking converts. There are no seminaries for training new leaders. There are no formal youth ministries, no printed discipleship courses, no public worship gatherings, no banners, no events, no conferences, no Christian bookstores, no church bulletins, and no public baptisms. And yet the church grows.

This reality forces a deeper reflection: what is truly essential for the kingdom of God to advance? Iran's revival demonstrates that Christ builds His church through the power of the Spirit, the spreading of the gospel message, the Scriptures, and courageous discipleship - not through external structures alone.

House-church networks operate with remarkable simplicity. A typical gathering may involve five to fifteen believers meeting after dark in a living room, a basement, or a rooftop. They arrive separately, often at staggered intervals. Windows are covered. Voices remain low. Phones are switched off or placed in another room to avoid surveillance. A simple meal or tea may be shared. Then the group reads Scripture aloud, discusses what it means, and prays for each other.

church Leadership is fluid and relational, not formal. The most spiritually mature believer in the group often takes responsibility for teaching the Bible. That person may have little formal theological training, but they have deep faith, perseverance, and a willingness to risk their freedom for the sake of the gospel. As the church multiplies, new believers quickly become leaders themselves. They are discipled with urgency because persecution demands it.

They learn to read Scripture deeply, to pray fervently, and to share their faith cautiously but boldly. This form of discipleship mirrors the New Testament more closely than many modern models. The early church also met in homes, under threat, with simple rhythms of Scripture, the breaking of bread, fellowship, and prayer.

The Apostle Paul could also not rely on church buildings or seminaries in his day; he relied on the Holy Spirit working through communities of faith that met quietly in houses and grew through relationships. Iran's underground church is a living reminder that the gospel thrives when believers take responsibility for one another's spiritual growth.

When baptism requires a desert or a bathtub

In Iran, baptism is one of the most dangerous acts a person can undertake. It's not just a spiritual symbol; it is a legal declaration that can trigger severe punishment. For this reason, baptisms often take place in extreme secrecy. Some occur in the middle of the night in private bathrooms, using showers or small tubs. Others happen in remote outdoor locations - mountain streams, empty beaches along the Caspian Sea, or secluded sections of the desert where no one is watching.

A new believer might be discipled for several months before being baptised. This is not out of reluctance, but caution. Leaders want to ensure that the person understands the seriousness of their commitment and the risks involved. When the moment comes, the baptism is deeply moving. Tears flow freely. Prayers are whispered through trembling voices. The sense of the sacred is overwhelming. Many Iranian believers later describe their baptism as the most powerful moment of their lives, more profound than they ever imagined.

This hidden sacrament echoes the biblical simplicity of baptism: an act of obedience, a sign of new life, a declaration that Jesus is Lord. In Iran, that declaration comes at great cost. But it also comes with great joy. Baptism becomes not just a ceremony but a courageous proclamation of identity: *"I belong to Christ."* And the church rejoices.

Control, crackdowns, and contradictions

The Iranian government views Christianity, and particularly conversion from Islam, as a serious threat to their national identity and political stability. Because of this, the regime invests considerable resources in suppressing the underground church. Intelligence agents monitor online communications, track suspected house-church leaders, infiltrate Christian networks, and pressure families to reject converted relatives. Arrests, interrogations, beatings, imprisonment, and long sentences are common.

Despite these crackdowns, the authorities face a paradox. The more they suppress Christianity, the more it grows. Many Iranians, especially younger generations, interpret the harsh treatment of Christians as evidence that the state fears the message of Jesus. Persecution inadvertently validates the gospel. When people see believers willing to endure hardship for their faith, they conclude that Christianity must offer something worth suffering for.

This paradox echoes the early church. In the Book of Acts, persecution scattered believers, but everywhere they went they preached the word. The same appears to be happening in Iran: hostility fuels hunger, and repression gives rise to resilience. A church refined by fire emerges stronger, not weaker.

Furthermore, the regime cannot easily control digital platforms. Despite strict censorship, millions of Iranians use VPNs to access news, social media, and Christian content. The very tools intended to silence dissent become channels for the gospel.

A nation in spiritual flux

Understanding Iran's revival requires recognising the spiritual dissatisfaction widespread among Iranians today. While Islam remains publicly dominant, many are privately questioning its authority. Younger generations often feel disconnected from the religious ideology of the regime. They see the deep hypocrisy of certain religious leaders.

They witness corruption, privilege, and injustice. They feel the weight of laws that restrict personal freedom. Over time, these frustrations create spiritual disillusionment.

Into this disillusionment, the message of Jesus enters with profound resonance. The gospel offers grace instead of legalism, forgiveness instead of fear, relationship instead of ritual, and hope instead of despair. The teachings of Jesus Christ, especially His compassion, His healing power, and His emphasis on love, speak deeply to Iranians searching for something real.

An increasing number of Iranians are privately rejecting religion altogether. Yet many of these "nones" are not opposed to faith, they are opposed to oppressive religion. When they encounter Christianity through a friend, a dream, or a digital broadcast, the contrast is stark. Jesus is not another authority figure demanding obedience; He is the Saviour who gave His life for them. This message, simple and ancient, is transforming the hearts of a modern nation.

Iran in the context of global renewal

As surprising as Iran's revival might seem, it is part of a broader pattern of God's activity in the world. Around the globe, in places where Christian faith is marginalised or persecuted, the church is growing rapidly. Iran joins China, Afghanistan, parts of India, and segments of the Muslim world in witnessing extraordinary spiritual hunger. In many of these contexts, visions, dreams, and supernatural encounters are reported with striking frequency.

At the same time, Western countries - despite spiritual decline in some sectors - are also now experiencing pockets of renewal: university revivals, prayer movements, multicultural church planting, and a renewed hunger for Scripture. The Asbury Outpouring in the United States serves as a parallel example of how God is awakening young people in unexpected places. Iran's awakening therefore stands as a powerful reminder: the Holy Spirit of God is not bound by geography, politics, culture, or ideology.

He moves freely, sovereignly, and beautifully across the earth. The same Jesus who walked through the streets of Galilee now walks through the alleys of Tehran. The same Spirit who filled the upper room fills living rooms in Mashhad and Shiraz. The same gospel that turned the world upside down in the first century is doing the same in a nation where many thought it impossible.

The courage to say "Yes" to Jesus

Perhaps the most remarkable element of Iran's current revival is the great courage displayed by ordinary believers. Every act of discipleship requires bravery: gathering to worship, reading Scripture, sharing faith, baptising new converts, and even praying together. Yet the Iranian church continues to grow because men and women - from teenagers to grandparents - have chosen to follow Jesus no matter the cost.

Their courage challenges the global church. In places where Christianity is comfortable, believers may forget the weight of Jesus' words: *"Whoever wants to be my disciple must deny themselves and take up their cross and follow me."* (Matthew 16:24). Iranian Christians live those words daily. Their faithfulness serves as a living sermon to the world.

What is happening in Iran is not a fleeting phenomenon. It is a sustained move of God, forged in adversity, rooted in Scripture, fuelled by prayer, and carried by courage. It is one of the most significant spiritual awakenings of the twenty-first century - a reminder that God is at work in places we least expect, drawing people to Himself with irresistible grace.

And the story is far from over.

3. DREAMS, VISIONS, MIRACLES AND MUSLIMS

Across the Muslim world - from Morocco to Indonesia, from Turkey to Pakistan, from the Gulf states to remote villages in North Africa - a remarkable phenomenon has quietly unfolded over recent decades. Men and women from Islamic backgrounds are encountering Jesus in dreams, visions, and supernatural experiences. These encounters are not isolated or anecdotal. They are documented in many missionary reports, academic case studies, refugee interviews, field research, and testimonies gathered across multiple continents. The sheer volume and consistency of these stories demand thoughtful, sober attention.

This chapter does not aim to sensationalise or exaggerate. Rather, it seeks to explore a pattern that has become one of the most striking features of global Christian growth: Millions of Muslims encountering Christ in ways that bypass all cultural, religious, and geographical barriers.

These encounters will often occur in contexts where access to Scripture is limited, where evangelism is illegal, and where Christian communities are persecuted or underground. In such places, God appears to be revealing Himself in ways that echo the stories of Scripture.

A spiritual climate prepared for revelation

The Islamic world is vast, diverse, and deeply spiritual. For many Muslims, dreams carry significant cultural and spiritual weight. Throughout all of Islamic history, dreams have been considered meaningful. Even today, many Muslims believe that God can guide, warn, or speak through dreams. This belief forms part of the spiritual soil into which God has sown some amazing revelations of Jesus Christ.

In many predominantly Muslim societies, access to Christian teaching is severely restricted. churches are scarce. Bibles may be banned. Being seen with a Christian friend can provoke suspicion or danger.

Converting to Christianity can result in imprisonment, beatings, loss of employment, or expulsion from one's family. In some contexts, conversion carries a death sentence. Under such conditions, the traditional means of evangelism are nearly impossible.

And yet, in these very environments, millions of Muslims have reported encounters with a man in white – who is compassionate and radiant and authoritative. He is also calling them by name, inviting them to follow Him, or revealing Himself as *"the Way, the Truth, and the Life."* Many later discover that the man they saw is Jesus Christ.

These encounters do not replace Scripture; they lead people to Scripture. They do not bypass the gospel; they draw people toward it. They do not eliminate the need for Christian community; they awaken a deep hunger for it.

A man in white: The testimony of millions

One of the most common features of these testimonies is the appearance of this "man in white." Across languages, cultures, and regions, the descriptions are remarkably similar. People speak of a radiant figure, clothed in shining white garments, filled with light, full of compassion. Some see Him standing by their bed. Others see Him in a dream, walking toward them or reaching out His hands. Some hear Him speak; others experience His presence silently yet unmistakably.

What makes these encounters compelling is their consistency. These are not the stories of one culture or tribe. They come from Arabs in the Middle East, Kurds in northern Iraq, Berbers in North Africa, Pashtuns in Afghanistan, Persians in Iran, and migrants in Europe.

Many of the individuals who report these dreams have never read the Bible, never met a Christian, and have no prior knowledge of Christian theology. Yet they describe Jesus in terms that align closely with the New Testament depiction of Him.

Some recount hearing Him say words from Scripture - words they later discover in the Bible. Others describe being enveloped in a love unlike anything they have ever known. A few speak of physical healings, deliverance from fear, or a sudden sense of peace that remained long after the dream. These testimonies display a recurring pattern:

1. *A supernatural encounter* - through a dream, vision, or unmistakable voice.

2. *A revelation of Jesus* - as Lord, Saviour, or Shepherd.

3. *A deep conviction of sin* or spiritual emptiness.

4. *A desire to find a Bible* or meet a Christian.

Transformation evidenced by courage, joy, and new faith.

What makes these encounters so powerful is not merely the experience itself but the fruit that follows. People once hostile to Christianity begin searching for the gospel. Those bound by fear find true freedom. Those living under heavy spiritual oppression experience peace. Those who have never held a Bible begin seeking one with urgency.

Dreams that lead to desert streams

In North Africa, a young man recounted a dream in which he was walking through a desert, thirsty and exhausted. Suddenly, a man in white appeared and said, *"Follow Me."* The man led him to a stream of water flowing through the sand. When he awoke, he began searching online for the identity of the man in his dream. After weeks of searching, he found a Christian radio station broadcasting in his language. The preacher spoke about Jesus, the Living Water. The young man wept as he realised that the man he saw in his dream was Christ.

This pattern has been repeated countless times. Dreams often serve as a doorway, an invitation. They awaken a thirst that leads people to living water. They stir curiosity that leads to discovery. They break down barriers of fear and open hearts to truth. Many missionaries report encountering many people who have been prepared by dreams long before they meet a Christian.

In remote villages, entire families have experienced identical dreams on the same night. In refugee camps, groups of seekers have gathered after seeing visions of Jesus. In cities, individuals have travelled long distances seeking someone who can explain the dream they had. The Spirit of God is moving in ways that defy conventional methods.

The role of Scripture in confirming the vision

While dreams often initiate the journey, Scripture grounds and confirms it. Many Muslims who encounter Jesus supernaturally later describe their shock when they open the New Testament for the first time and find the same Jesus they saw in their dream. They recognise His voice, His character, His compassion, His authority.

Passages such as these are especially transformative:

"I am the good shepherd." (John 10:11)
"I am the way and the truth and the life." (John 14:6)
"I am the light of the world." (John 8:12)
"Come to me, all you who are weary and burdened." (Matthew 11:28)

These verses often match the imagery and words they heard in their dreams. This confirmation becomes life-changing. Dreams may awaken, but Scripture reveals. Dreams may call, but Scripture explains. Dreams may lead someone to seek Jesus, but Scripture teaches them who He truly is.

This is consistent with how God has always worked throughout salvation history. Dreams point; the Word directs. Visions stir; the gospel transforms.

Encounters that bring healing and deliverance

Another striking feature of this movement is the number of testimonies involving healing or deliverance. Many Muslims come from contexts where spiritual oppression is very real - fear, nightmares, curses, or bondage to unclean spirits. In numerous cases, an encounter with Jesus in a dream leads to immediate relief from spiritual torment.

One woman in the Middle East described years of nightmares and overwhelming fear. After dreaming of Jesus placing His hand on her head and saying, *"You are Mine,"* she awoke in peace for the first time in years. That morning, she prayed, *"Jesus, I want to follow You."* These stories echo the ministry of Jesus recorded in the Gospels. He healed the sick, calmed storms, freed the oppressed, and spoke peace. When He draws near n dreams or visions, the same authority accompanies Him.

Why is this happening now?

This phenomenon has accelerated in recent decades. Several factors help explain why:

1. *Restricted access to the gospel*
   In places where evangelism is outlawed, God often works directly in ways that bypass barriers.

2. *Widespread disillusionment with religion*
   Many Muslims have grown weary of the political and cultural weight of religion; they hunger for a personal encounter with God.

3. *The availability of digital Scripture and Christian media*
   Dreams spark curiosity, and digital access allows seekers to find the gospel quietly and quickly.

4. *A sovereign move of God*
   Ultimately, this is the most significant factor. God is revealing His Son in ways that echo the book of Acts.

As one missionary put it, "We are witnessing what many believe to be the greatest turning of Muslims to Christ in history."
The next section will explore the theological significance of this phenomenon and how it connects to the wider story of God's work across nations.

The theology of revelation: How God makes Himself known

The widespread phenomenon of Muslims encountering Jesus in dreams and visions raises profound theological questions. How does God reveal Himself? Why does He choose certain times, places, or methods?

What is the relationship between supernatural encounters and Scripture? How should the global church interpret these extraordinary accounts?

Throughout the Bible, God reveals Himself in a variety of ways. He speaks through creation (Psalm 19:1-4), through prophets, through His written Word, through His Son, and through the Holy Spirit. He speaks through circumstances, through the church, through miracles, and at times through dreams and visions. These modes of revelation are not in competition; they complement one another. Scripture remains the authoritative revelation of God's truth, yet God in His sovereignty often uses dreams or visions as part of His redemptive work.

From Genesis through to Revelation, dreams and visions appear as a significant thread in the tapestry of God's communication with humanity.

- Joseph interpreted dreams in Egypt.
- Daniel interpreted dreams in Babylon.
- Joseph, the husband of Mary, was guided by dreams concerning the protection of Jesus.
- Peter received a vision that prepared him to bring the gospel to the Gentiles (Acts 10:10-16).
- Paul's conversion involved a supernatural encounter that redirected his entire life (Acts 9:3-6).
- John received the book of Revelation through visions given by the Spirit.

Theologically, then, the appearance of Christ to Muslims in dreams is not unprecedented. Instead, it aligns with a long biblical pattern: God reveals Himself uniquely in times and places where His written Word is restricted, resisted, or persecuted. In many contexts of the Muslim world, believers have little or no access to Scripture, Christian fellowship, or gospel preaching. God meets them where they are, using means that cannot be monitored, censored, or blocked.

Dreams, visions, and supernatural encounters are not ends in themselves. They function as signposts pointing toward Jesus, who is revealed fully in Scripture. They awaken the heart, draw the seeker into the gospel story, and prepare them to respond in faith. The Spirit stirs spiritual hunger, and the Word satisfies it.

Why Jesus appears in persecuted contexts

One striking observation about this global phenomenon is that it is most prevalent in places where following Jesus Christ comes at great personal cost. This is not a coincidence. God often reveals Himself most powerfully in places of profound suffering or spiritual oppression. The biblical pattern is clear: God is near to the oppressed, close to the broken-hearted, and present with those in danger.

In countries where conversion from Islam is punishable by imprisonment, violence, or even death, the stakes are incredibly high. To follow Jesus requires courage, sacrifice, and conviction. When God reveals Himself to someone in a dream, He often plants in them a boldness that cannot be explained by human psychology alone. They have encountered the living Christ. Such encounters produce resilient disciples. This reality echoes the experience of the early church. Under Roman persecution, Jesus often revealed Himself supernaturally to sustain and guide His people. The same pattern continues today. Where the cost is highest, God often moves with the greatest clarity.

These encounters also undermine oppressive spiritual systems. In societies where religious leaders claim exclusive access to truth, a dream of Jesus bypasses those human power structures. It empowers individuals to seek truth directly from God rather than through coercive religious systems imposed upon them.

The ripple effect: How one dream becomes a movement

A dream does not simply change an individual. In many cases, it transforms families and entire communities. In the Muslim world, communal identity is very strong. Decisions are rarely individualistic.

When one person becomes a follower of Jesus, others in the household often examine the testimony, test its truth, and may come to faith themselves. A single dream can set off a chain reaction:

- A man sees Jesus in a dream, begins searching for answers, and meets a Christian who shares the gospel.
- His wife notices the transformation in his character and begins reading Scripture alongside him.
- Their children ask why their parents are different, and they too become curious.
- The family begins gathering with other believers quietly in their home.
- A house church is born.

Sometimes the sequence happens in reverse. A child or a mother has a dream, and the father - initially resistant - becomes curious. In some cases, entire family units surrender to Christ within a short period. This is not common in individualistic Western contexts, but it is a normal dynamic in collectivist cultures.

Dreams also create bridges between the Muslim world and the global church. Converts who flee persecution often arrive in refugee camps or Western nations with a burning desire to find Christians. Many tell pastors or missionaries, *"I saw Jesus in a dream,"* or *"A man in white told me to find people who follow Him."*

These encounters become testimonies that inspire and encourage believers worldwide, reminding the global church that God is actively working in places where mission strategies are restricted.

The apologetic force of dreams and visions

From an apologetic perspective, the consistency and fruit of these supernatural encounters challenge sceptical assumptions. Critics often dismiss such phenomena as psychological projections, wishful thinking, or cultural imagination.

However, the global spread and thematic uniformity of these testimonies make such explanations insufficient. Consider these several factors:

1. *Geographical diversity*
   The encounters occur in nations with vastly different cultures, languages, and levels of exposure to Christianity.

2. *Lack of prior knowledge*
   Many who experience these dreams have never heard Christian teachings about Jesus' divinity, His voice, or His appearance.

3. *The fruit of transformation*
   These encounters produce dramatic spiritual and moral change - repentance, love, forgiveness, peace-making, and devotion to Christ.

4. *The willingness to suffer*
   Many respond to these dreams by embracing a faith that could cost them everything. This response is difficult to explain psychologically.

5. *Consistency of imagery*
   The recurring motif of a radiant man in white appears in testimonies separated by thousands of miles and differing cultural backgrounds.

These factors create a compelling case that these encounters cannot be dismissed merely as subjective or symbolic. Something real is happening — something that aligns with biblical patterns of divine revelation and produces lasting transformation.

The church's role: Confirming, discipling, and sending

While dreams often initiate the journey to faith, the church plays an essential role in confirming and nurturing these new believers. After an encounter, a Muslim seeker frequently feels compelled to find a Christian or obtain a Bible. Many describe a deep inner urging they can't ignore. When they meet a believer, the church becomes an interpretive community through which the dream finds meaning.

The early church functioned this way. When Saul encountered Christ in a blinding vision, it was Ananias who confirmed the encounter, prayed for him, baptised him, and welcomed him into the community of faith (Acts 9:10–18). The Spirit and the church work together. The church's role today mirrors that pattern:

- *Confirming* the authenticity of the encounter through Scripture
- *Discipling* new believers in foundations of faith
- *Providing community* and spiritual family
- *Training leaders* to serve in underground networks
- *Equipping* them for the risks ahead
- *Sending* them back into their communities as ambassadors for Christ

This strong partnership between divine revelation and human discipleship is central to sustained revival. God awakens hearts, the church nurtures them, and the gospel spreads.

When the Holy Spirit crosses borders

One of the most astonishing realities of this movement is that dreams and visions cross geographic borders effortlessly. Where missionaries cannot enter, the Spirit enters. Where Bibles are banned, the Word of God appears in a dream. Where churches cannot gather, Jesus Himself gathers seekers in visions and calls them by name.

This phenomenon reveals the global heart of God. He is drawing Muslims to Himself not reluctantly but eagerly. He is revealing His Son to those who have never heard His name spoken in love. He is breaking chains of fear and oppression. He is bringing light into places long overshadowed by darkness.

The revival among Muslims is not an anomaly - it is a move of God consistent with His character, His mission, and His promise that the gospel will reach every tribe, language, people, and nation. And it is only the beginning.

Stories from the frontlines: Testimonies that defy borders

Throughout the Muslim world, stories of these amazing dreams and visions continue to emerge - quiet, personal, yet profoundly transformative testimonies that defy borders, regimes, and expectations. While every story is unique, the similarities between them form a powerful tapestry of God's activity in places where missionary access is limited and Christian presence is severely restricted. These testimonies shine light into regions often perceived as spiritually unreachable.

In the Arabian Peninsula, a woman raised in a strict Islamic household described a dream that altered the course of her life. Years of depression, loneliness, and fear had weighed heavily on her. One night, she dreamt of a man standing in brilliant light. He spoke her name tenderly, as though He had known her since birth. *"Come, follow Me,"* He said, extending His hand. She awoke with tears streaming down her face. For the first time in her life, she felt safe.

Over the following weeks, she searched secretly online, found Christian teaching in Arabic, and eventually obtained a digital New Testament. Reading the words of Jesus, she recognised the voice she had heard in her dream. Months later, she was baptised by two Christian women who met with her in a private home. Her life changed dramatically - hope replaced despair, and courage replaced fear.

In North Africa, a former imam recounted how he had devoted his life to studying Islamic law. He had risen in influence within his community and was respected for his knowledge and piety. Yet he struggled with deep spiritual emptiness. One night, he dreamt that he was in a crowded marketplace. A man in white approached him, took him by the hand, and said, *"You are mine."* The imam tried to speak but found himself overwhelmed by the man's presence.

Upon waking, he felt compelled to read the Injil—the New Testament that Islam acknowledges but generally discourages Muslims from reading.

He obtained a copy through a friend, and as he read the Gospels, he encountered the same voice he had heard in his dream. After months of inner struggle, he surrendered his life to Jesus. Today, he leads a small house - church, discipling new believers under constant threat of arrest.

In Southeast Asia, a young migrant worker living in poverty had long felt abandoned and forgotten. His life was marked by exploitation, isolation, and a sense of worthlessness. One night, Jesus appeared to him in a dream and said, *"I am with you."* The next day, a co-worker invited him to a secret Bible study. When he entered the room, he saw a painting of Jesus on the wall - the same face he had seen in his dream. Overcome by emotion, he fell to the floor and wept. He later said, *"I thought I was nobody, but Jesus came to me."* Today, he serves quietly among migrant communities, sharing his hope with others.

Such stories are not rare - they are multiplying. Thousands of similar testimonies have been recorded by many missionaries, researchers, refugee pastors, and Christian broadcasters. While each story has its own particular details, the central theme remains consistent: Jesus is revealing Himself to Muslims in deeply personal and unmistakably supernatural ways.

The role of suffering in awakening spiritual hunger

In many Muslim-majority countries, suffering is widespread - sometimes due to political instability, sometimes due to war, sometimes due to economic hardship, and often due to oppression or religious pressure.

While suffering is never desired or celebrated, Scripture shows repeatedly that God meets people in their deepest pain. When earthly hope collapses, spiritual hunger rises.

In the Middle East, decades of conflict have shattered families, cities, and entire nations. Refugee camps stretch across borders. Trauma is commonplace. Many who once clung tightly to their inherited faith now find themselves questioning everything. In this vacuum of despair, dreams of Jesus often come as a lifeline.

Refugee pastors recount stories of men and women who saw Jesus in a dream while sleeping in tents, on cold floors, or amid bombed-out ruins. These encounters come not as rebukes but as invitations - gentle, compassionate calls to life and hope.

In regions of Africa where extremist groups terrorise villagers, some believers testify that Jesus appeared to them before an attack, warning them to flee. Others describe miraculous deliverance during captivity. Still others report seeing visions that strengthen them to endure suffering. These testimonies mirror biblical accounts where God guided Joseph, Daniel, Paul, and others in times of danger.

Suffering does not hinder God's work. In many cases, it becomes the very soil in which the seeds of faith take root. Jesus often reveals Himself to the broken, the oppressed, and the displaced. He comes as the Healer, the Shepherd, the Prince of Peace. In contexts where earthly hope is scarce, heavenly hope shines brightest.

The quiet movement among the youth

One of the most surprising dimensions of this phenomenon is the number of young Muslims encountering Christ in dreams. Many of these young people live in societies where questioning tradition is discouraged, where religious identity is woven into family honour, and where apostasy is considered shameful or dangerous. Yet despite these pressures, God is touching the hearts of young men and women with striking clarity.

A teenage boy in the Middle East told a Pastor, *"I saw Jesus in my dream. He told me to read the words in the book no one in my family is allowed to read."* He went on to describe how he searched online until he found a digital copy of the New Testament.

His parents later noticed the transformation in his character - kindness replacing anger, peace replacing anxiety - but could not explain the change. Eventually, his mother asked what had happened. When he shared the story, she wept and said, *"I had the same dream."*

In Central Asia, a young woman studying at university dreamt that she was drowning in a river. A man in white pulled her out and said, *"I have rescued you."* She awoke terrified yet strangely comforted. Weeks later, she attended a secret Christian gathering and heard a believer describe Jesus as the One who rescues us from sin and death. She immediately realised that the dream had been a call from God. She surrendered her life to Christ that night.

These stories demonstrate that God is moving powerfully among the younger generation. So many young Muslims really long for authenticity. They question the religious formalism of their societies. They crave real encounters with God, not rigid rituals or oppressive traditions. When Jesus appears, He meets them at the deepest point of their longing.

Visions that lead to forgiveness

A recurring theme in testimonies across the Muslim world is the experience of profound forgiveness. Many who encounter Jesus describe being overwhelmed by His love - a love that dissolves bitterness, resentment, and fear. This is particularly striking in regions marked by ethnic or sectarian conflict.

In one nation marked by decades of religious tension, a former militant recounted how he had hated Christians for years. One night, he dreamt of Jesus standing before him with open arms. The man fell to his knees and wept. In the dream, Jesus said, *"You are forgiven."* When he awakened, he felt a peace he had never known. He sought out a Christian, confessed his past, and began a new life in Christ. Today, he works to bring reconciliation in his community.

Forgiveness is one of the most powerful evidences of Christ's presence. It is not natural for people driven by hatred or trauma to suddenly embrace reconciliation. But when Jesus reveals Himself, He transforms the hardest hearts. His forgiveness breaks cycles of vengeance and gives birth to healing. This, too, reflects the gospel: *"If the Son sets you free, you will be free indeed."* (John 8:36).

Visions in restricted nations: When Jesus enters a prison

Perhaps the most dramatic testimonies come from believers who encountered Jesus in prisons or detention centres. In some regions, Christians who convert from Islam are arrested, interrogated, or isolated. Yet in these dark places, Jesus often appears with luminous clarity.

One man imprisoned for sharing the gospel described how he heard singing in his cell at night. When he opened his eyes, he saw Jesus standing beside him, radiant with light, speaking words of comfort. The man later said, *"I was not alone. Christ was with me, and I feared nothing."* After his release, his testimony helped many others come to Christ.

In another country, a woman detained for her conversion described a vision in which Jesus touched her bruises and said, *"I am with you always."* Her wounds healed unexpectedly quickly, and she boldly shared her faith with fellow prisoners.

These testimonies echo the story in Acts 16:25-26, where Paul and Silas were in prison and God's presence broke their chains, opened doors, and turned suffering into salvation. Jesus enters the prison cells of the twenty-first century just as He did in the first century.

A global pattern of Divine pursuit

The more these stories are gathered, analysed, and compared, the clearer the pattern becomes. God is actively pursuing Muslims across the world. He is revealing His Son to those who least expect it, in places least open to Christian witness, and through means no government can stop.

This is not a fringe phenomenon - it is a widespread, sustained move of God. It is a sign of His mercy, His sovereignty, and His unstoppable mission to draw all people to Himself.

The Spirit is moving across deserts, cities, mountains, villages, and refugee camps, calling men and women into His kingdom.

How dreams and visions are reshaping the global church

The rise of dreams and visions among Muslims has not only transformed individual lives - it has reshaped the global church in profound ways.

Pastors, missionaries, theologians, and mission agencies have had to rethink their assumptions about how God works, how people come to faith, and how discipleship must adapt in a world where divine revelation often precedes human witness.

For generations, many Christians have assumed that evangelism flowed primarily in one direction - from the Western church to the rest of the world. But in recent decades, the flow has reversed. The Holy Spirit Himself appears to be taking the lead in regions where traditional mission efforts are blocked. Instead of missionaries creating opportunities for the gospel, dreams are prompting seekers to ask questions long before they meet a believer. This inversion challenges the church to recognise that God is not bound by our strategies.

Mission leaders increasingly describe their role not as initiating gospel conversations but as responding to the work that God has already begun. Instead of pushing open locked doors, they are finding that God has unlocked them from the inside.

This shift carries deep theological significance. It reminds the church that mission is not primarily a human enterprise. It is God's mission. We participate in a story already unfolding - a story in which the Spirit goes ahead of us, preparing hearts, breaking down barriers, and revealing Christ in ways beyond our imagination.

The church learns to listen

One of the most transformative lessons the global church has learned from this movement is the importance of listening. In many cases, missionaries have been surprised to discover that seekers knew far more about Jesus than expected - because He had already appeared to them.

A missionary in the Middle East recounted meeting a man who said, *"Jesus told me you would come."* The missionary had never shared this story publicly, because it sounded unbelievable. But he could not deny what he had heard. When he asked the man to explain, the man described a dream in which Jesus had shown him the face of a stranger who would teach him the way of salvation. Days later, that stranger knocked on his door. The missionary wept as he realised that he was witnessing something far larger than himself.

These moments force believers to listen carefully - to God's leading, to the stories of seekers, and to the quiet movements of the Spirit. The posture of listening replaces the posture of control. The church becomes a partner in God's work rather than the architect of it.

Listening also becomes essential in discipleship. New believers often carry a rich understanding of the character of Jesus from their dreams, but little knowledge of Scripture or Christian doctrine. Missionaries have found that they must build discipleship around the seeker's encounter with Christ - not dismissing it but grounding it in the Scriptures. This requires humility, discernment, and sensitivity to the Spirit.

From dreams to discipleship networks

While dreams may bring people to Christ, they cannot disciple them. The church must step into that role. One of the most extraordinary developments in recent years is the emergence of discipleship networks among Muslim-background believers. These networks operate quietly, often digitally, sometimes in person, and occasionally across borders. A typical pathway looks like this:

1. A seeker experiences a dream or vision of Jesus.

2. The seeker searches online for Christian content.

3. They encounter a digital Bible, a Christian broadcast, or an underground believer.

4. They are connected to a small discipleship group, either local or virtual.

5. They begin reading the New Testament with others, often starting with the Gospels.

6. They are baptised in secret when ready.

7. Many become leaders of new groups within months.

This rapid multiplication surprises Western Christians who associate discipleship with long-term programs or highly structured curricula. But in persecuted contexts, discipleship is urgent. Believers must mature quickly, because they may soon lead others or face persecution themselves.

The growth of these networks has contributed to explosive church expansion in countries where Christianity is officially restricted. While the exact numbers are difficult to verify, many mission researchers believe that millions of Muslims worldwide have come to Christ in the past two decades - far more than in the previous millennium.

When persecution cannot stop the gospel

Persecution plays a paradoxical role in this movement. It forces the church underground, yet strengthens its resolve. It limits public gatherings, yet intensifies private devotion. It silences public preaching, yet repeatedly fails to silence the testimonies of believers who have seen Jesus in dreams.

In some nations, believers regularly meet in forests, mountains, or abandoned buildings under cover of darkness. In others, they gather in small apartments, rotating locations to avoid suspicion. Some rely on encrypted apps to share prayer requests. Others memorise Scripture because digital Bibles are too dangerous to keep. Despite these challenges, the church continues to grow. In fact, persecution often becomes a catalyst rather than a deterrent. Many Muslim-background believers testify that suffering deepens their faith. They see persecution not as a curse but as a confirmation that they belong to Christ.

This mirrors the early church. The book of Acts shows that persecution scattered believers, but everywhere they went they proclaimed the word of God with boldness. The same pattern holds true today. Where suffering increases, courage rises. Where fear seeks to silence the church, dreams stoke conviction. Persecution, rather than stopping revival, frequently fuels it.

The impact on Muslim communities

The ripple effect of these Divine encounters extends far beyond individuals. As more Muslims come to Christ, family dynamics shift, communities change, and the deep cultural perceptions of Christianity begin to soften. In many regions, Christianity is misunderstood or misrepresented. But when a family member encounters Jesus personally, misconceptions begin to crumble.

A father who once forbade his children from hearing the gospel may suddenly question the spiritual truth he built his life upon. A mother who sees her daughter transformed by Jesus may begin reading Scripture secretly. A sibling who witnesses the peace of Christ in a persecuted relative may quietly begin seeking God.

In some communities, small clusters of believers develop which are connected by trust rather than geography. They support each other, pray for one another, and share resources with each other. Some communities even reframe their cultural identity around their new faith - seeing themselves not as abandoning their heritage, but as discovering its fulfilment in Christ. The transformation is slow, delicate, and often messy. But it is real.

Miracles that lead to mission

Another fascinating development is the emergence of Muslim-background evangelists and missionaries. Many who encounter Jesus in dreams feel compelled to share their testimony with others. Despite danger, they boldly proclaim the gospel to family, friends, neighbours, and sometimes even strangers. These believers carry a unique authority. Their testimony resonates deeply with other Muslims because they share the same cultural background, language, and religious experiences.

They can speak to the spiritual thirst of their communities with authenticity. Their courage inspires many others. Their faith is contagious. Some become itinerant evangelists within their country, travelling quietly from one region to another.

Others become digital missionaries, sharing their stories online, participating in encrypted Bible studies, or answering questions from seekers. Still others cross borders, carrying the gospel into refugee camps, migrant communities, and diaspora churches.

In a remarkable twist of divine strategy, many missionaries to the Muslim world today are former Muslims themselves. Their testimonies bridge gaps that traditional mission work cannot. Their stories become seeds of faith in places where the gospel has never been heard.

Dreams and global mission strategy

The rise of dreams and visions has profoundly affected mission strategy worldwide. Many mission organisations have shifted from traditional evangelism models to partnership-based, disciple-making approaches that emphasise:

- Listening to the Spirit
- Responding to the work God has already begun
- Empowering local believers
- Operating in small, flexible cell structures
- Prioritising Scripture engagement
- Discipling entire households
- Training leaders from within movements
- Relying on prayer more than programmes

Dreams often serve as the initial bridge. Missionaries increasingly describe their work not as initiating the movement of God but as recognising it. Their task is to build discipleship around the encounters God has already given. This shift has produced unexpected results.

In many regions, Christian growth is now faster than at any time in modern history — not because of sophisticated strategies, but because the Spirit is moving ahead of the church.

The future of this movement

As we look toward the coming decades, it is almost certain that dreams and visions will continue to play a significant role in God's work among Muslims. The geopolitical landscape remains complex, but God's mission remains unstoppable. The Spirit is not hindered by closed borders or authoritarian governments.

This phenomenon may even accelerate as more Muslims gain access to digital Scripture, online discipleship, and Christian global networks. As the church grows, so will the testimonies. As persecution increases, so will the courage of believers. As the world becomes more interconnected, stories of Jesus appearing in dreams will continue to spread - encouraging, inspiring, and challenging the global church.

This is a quiet revolution - born in bedrooms, refugee tents, prison cells, and remote villages. It is a movement of grace that stretches from the deserts of Arabia to the cities of Europe, from the mountains of Central Asia to the coastlines of North Africa. It is one of the most astonishing signs of God's activity in the twenty-first century. And it is reshaping the spiritual landscape of the Muslim world.

4. CHINA'S HOUSE-CHURCH MOVEMENT
FAITH UNDER FIRE

The story of the modern Chinese church is one of the greatest spiritual miracles to unfold in the last century. Few movements in Christian history have demonstrated such resilience, depth, creativity, and sacrificial faith. Under heavy surveillance, strict regulations, social pressure, and periods of intense persecution, the church in China has not merely survived - it has grown exponentially. What began as a scattered remnant in the 1950s after the expulsion of foreign missionaries has become a vast network of believers worshipping in homes, apartments, rural villages, factories, university dormitories, and urban high-rises.

This chapter explores a movement that has captured worldwide attention: a church without buildings, without seminaries, without public visibility - yet one filled with power, hunger, and astonishing courage. It is a church whose vibrancy rebukes the assumption that Christian growth depends on political freedom or institutional strength. Instead, it reveals what happens when ordinary believers devote themselves wholly to Jesus Christ in the midst of adversity.

The seeds of faith in a season of silence

To understand the present, we must first briefly revisit the past. When the Communist Party took power in 1949, China entered a new era. Christianity was seen by many officials as a Western influence which is incompatible with socialist ideology. Foreign missionaries were expelled. Many Chinese pastors and church leaders were imprisoned or sent to terrible labour camps. Public gatherings were restricted. Bibles became scarce. The Cultural Revolution of 1966–1976 intensified the pressure, as all religious expressions were targeted and forced underground.

To outside observers, it appeared that Christianity in China might disappear. churches were closed or repurposed. Crosses were torn down. Christian literature was confiscated. Many believers faced humiliation, interrogation, and re-education.

Yet what the world could not see was the quiet, determined faith that continued in homes, whispered in prayers, hidden in hearts. God was at work in the silence.

When the Cultural Revolution ended, China slowly reopened. To the astonishment of many, believers began to re-emerge - scattered, wounded, but alive and faithful. The gospel had survived in the shadows. In some villages, elderly Christians had preserved tattered pages of Scripture. In others, memories of Bible verses had sustained communities. The church had not only survived; it had grown. What the enemy intended to extinguish had instead become a fertile ground for revival.

This pattern echoes a timeless truth: nothing can prevent the advance of Christ's kingdom. Jesus declared, *"I will build my church, and the gates of Hades will not overcome it."* (Matthew 16:18). China's story stands as living proof.

The birth of the house-church movement

As China entered the late 1970s and 1980s, believers faced a question: how should the church gather in a nation that still maintained tight control over religion? Two parallel streams emerged. One was the government-registered church, known as the *Three-Self Patriotic Movement.* The other was the unregistered, underground house-church movement.

While the registered church provided a degree of public worship space, many believers felt convicted to remain independent. They longed for spiritual vitality, bold evangelism, biblical teaching, and freedom from political oversight. Meeting in homes was practical; it was also theological. It reflected the New Testament pattern of believers gathering in small, relational communities where faith could flourish despite opposition.

These house churches became hubs of spiritual life. In rural areas, gatherings often took place under the cover of night, in barns, courtyards, or simple mud-brick homes. In cities, groups met in cramped apartments with curtains drawn and lights dimmed.

Believers arrived quietly, often at different times to avoid suspicion. A single guitar or whispered prayers were enough to fill the room with worship.

Leadership in these churches was seldom formal. It emerged from spiritual maturity rather than academic qualification. Pastors and evangelists were often farmers, labourers, or factory workers - ordinary people empowered by extraordinary grace. They memorised Scripture because printed Bibles were scarce. They preached with boldness because they knew the cost of following Christ.

This decentralised structure allowed the church to grow rapidly. If one leader was arrested, others continued the work. If one gathering place was compromised, believers shifted to another. Persecution, instead of weakening the church, equipped it with adaptability and resilience.

Revival in the countryside

Many of China's most dramatic church growth stories began in rural provinces - Henan, Anhui, Zhejiang, and others. In the 1980s and 1990s, reports emerged of villages turning to Christ almost entirely. Healing, deliverance, and answered prayer played a significant role in this movement. In communities with limited medical access, believers prayed boldly for the sick. When healings occurred, entire families and villages became open to the gospel.

These revivals were marked by simplicity - Scripture, prayer, worship, and testimony. They had no microphones, there were no programmes, no marketing campaigns. Yet the Spirit moved with power. Evangelists travelled on foot or by bicycle between distant villages, carrying only a small bag with a Bible and a few notebooks. They faced much harassment, interrogation, and imprisonment, yet they pressed on with joy.

Stories circulated of believers walking for hours to attend a secret gathering. Others travelled through rain, snow, or darkness to hear the Word of God taught.

Their devotion was unwavering. They saw themselves as part of a spiritual lineage of suffering saints, strengthened by the words of Jesus: *"In this world you will have trouble. But take heart! I have overcome the world."* (John 16:33).

The rise of urban house-churches

As China modernised and millions migrated from rural villages to cities, the house-church movement followed. Urban house churches emerged in Beijing, Shanghai, Guangzhou, Chengdu, and many other growing cities. These urban fellowships were often composed of young professionals: teachers, engineers, entrepreneurs, university students. They met in apartments, office buildings, cafes, and even rented hotel rooms.

Urban house churches brought new energy and theological depth. Leaders had greater access to resources - digital Bibles, online teaching, theological training from overseas contacts. Worship became richer, discipleship more structured, and community life more vibrant. These churches also developed a renewed passion for missions. Many prayed about sending missionaries along the ancient Silk Road back through Central Asia - an echo of the vision known historically as the *"Back to Jerusalem"* movement.

At the same time, these congregations remained vulnerable. Surveillance tightened. Local authorities pressured landlords, monitored gatherings, and cracked down on unregistered meetings. Yet believers persisted. They adapted with creativity - splitting into smaller groups, meeting at varying times, or using encrypted communication platforms.

When the cross means persecution

Persecution in China has taken many forms - harassment, fines, eviction, confiscation of property, and imprisonment. Pastors have been detained for leading unregistered gatherings. Entire churches have been forced to close. Homes used for worship have been raided regularly. In some provinces, authorities have demolished crosses or pressured believers to publicly renounce their faith.

In recent years, certain well-known churches have experienced significant pressure. Leaders have been arrested, congregations dispersed, children barred from attending Christian activities, and worship spaces shut down. These events serve as reminders that the cost of following Christ in China remains high.

And yet, believers continue to gather. They meet quietly in small apartments. They pray in whispered tones. They share Scripture from memory. They disciple new believers very patiently and courageously. They do not seek comfort - they seek Christ.

Their witness echoes the early church. When the apostles were flogged for preaching the gospel, they rejoiced *"because they had been counted worthy of suffering disgrace for the Name."* (Acts 5:41). Chinese believers understand this verse with depth Western comfort rarely affords.

A church unbound by walls

What makes China's revival remarkable is how it reveals the heart of God. The gospel cannot be contained by political boundaries or ideological control. When buildings are taken away, the church grows in homes. When pastors are imprisoned, new leaders rise. When printed Bibles are banned, Scripture is memorised. When evangelism is strictly forbidden, testimonies spread quietly through relationships.

The church in China stands as a living illustration of God's promise: *"The word of God is not chained."* (2 Timothy 2:9). It moves freely in prisons, factories, universities, rice fields, and high-rise apartments. It transforms lives through whispered prayers and secret gatherings. It advances through courage forged in suffering and joy found in Christ alone.

Discipleship under pressure: church growth in the shadows

One of the most extraordinary features of the Chinese house-church movement is the depth of its discipleship. In many parts of the world, discipleship is structured around programmes, study guides, seminars, and weekly classes.

In China, discipleship has been forged in far harsher conditions. It is largely shaped by memorised Scripture, quiet gatherings, whispered prayers, and the ever-present risk of persecution. It is not merely educational - it is transformational.

Believers learn early that following Jesus will require courage. They understand that obedience may cost them their job, their home, or their freedom. As a result, discipleship is not viewed as optional or secondary. It becomes the lifeline of the church.

Every believer must grow, because every believer may one day be forced to stand alone. They need a faith that can survive interrogation, isolation, or even imprisonment. They need a relationship with Christ that runs deeper than fear.

This environment produces a certain kind of disciple - humble, bold, prayerful, resilient, and rooted in Scripture. Chinese believers often memorise large portions of the Bible because printed copies can be confiscated.

Some of these house churches encourage new believers to start memorising key passages immediately: the Sermon on the Mount, Romans 8, John 14–17, or entire epistles. This practice recalls the ancient desert fathers and early persecuted churches, where the Word of God was carried not in books but in hearts.

Prayer is another major cornerstone. In home gatherings, long periods of extended prayer are common. Believers intercede for persecuted brothers and sisters, for gospel advancement, and for wisdom in navigating government pressure. Prayer vigils often stretch late into the night. In rural areas, dawn prayers in fields or forests are not unusual, as believers rise early before work to seek God's presence in solitude.

This rhythm of Scripture and prayer produces a community shaped by spiritual depth rather than outward structure. They gather not for programmes, but for the presence of God. They do not seek comfort - they seek Christ.

The theology of suffering: Joy in the midst of hardship

The Chinese church has a profound theology of suffering shaped by decades of persecution. It is not viewed as something to be avoided at all costs, but as something God uses to refine faith. Many believers see suffering as part of their calling - an honour, not a burden. This perspective is rooted deeply in Scripture, especially passages such as:

"Consider it pure joy... whenever you face trials of many kinds." (James 1:2)

"This light and momentary trouble is achieving for us an eternal glory." (2 Corinthians 4:17)

"Do not be surprised at the fiery ordeal... as though something strange were happening to you." (1 Peter 4:12)

For Chinese believers, these verses are not theoretical ideals; they are daily realities. A pastor once said, *"Persecution is our spiritual university."* By this he meant that trials sharpen discernment, deepen reliance on God, and separate genuine faith from shallow belief.

Historically, the church fathers spoke of suffering as the seed of the church. Early Christians grew deep roots because their faith was tested. China reflects this same pattern. Believers do not romanticise suffering - many have endured hardships that are painful and unjust. Yet they interpret suffering in light of Christ's sacrifice, not in light of human despair. This theology gives them strength to endure and joy to persevere.

Leadership that grows from the ground up

Leadership in China's house churches is organic rather than institutional. Leaders emerge from the community, recognised for their faithfulness, humility, and spiritual maturity rather than academic degrees or formal training. In many cases, leaders are shaped through suffering. Those who endure persecution with grace often become pillars of the local fellowship.

This mirrors the early church, where elders and pastors were appointed based on their character and devotion rather than education alone. Many Chinese leaders have only minimal theological training, yet they possess a deep, intuitive understanding of Scripture - sharpened by decades of reading, memorising, and living out the Word.

Some networks do operate training centres or Bible schools in secret locations. These programmes are often intense, with students studying Scripture for many hours each day. They pray, fast, evangelise, and serve together. Their training is marked not only by teaching, but by suffering. Students may be arrested during training, yet they continue with joy, seeing themselves as part of Christ's mission to China.

This ground-up leadership model has allowed the church to multiply quickly. When one leader is arrested or targeted, others quietly step in. When a house church is shut down, believers regroup in smaller clusters. The decentralised model makes it impossible for authorities to destroy the movement entirely.

Women at the heart of the movement

Like Iran's underground church, the Chinese house-church movement includes a remarkable number of women who are in leadership. Many are evangelists, pastors, disciple-makers, and prayer warriors. Their courage and faithfulness have shaped the church at every level.

In rural areas, women have often been the first to gather neighbours for prayer or Bible study. Many have started small churches in their homes. Their hospitality becomes a doorway for the gospel. Their daily rhythms of prayer anchor the spiritual life of their communities.

In urban fellowships, women serve as teachers, counsellors, worship leaders, and ministry coordinators. They play a central role in discipling younger believers and nurturing spiritual growth.

This prominence reflects the biblical pattern: Lydia opening her home to believers in Philippi; Priscilla teaching Apollos with theological precision; Mary, Phoebe, and others serving as early leaders in the church. In China, as in the New Testament, God uses women powerfully in His kingdom.

Evangelism in a restricted society

Evangelism in China requires great creativity, courage, and discernment. House-church believers do not rely on large events or public preaching. Instead, they share Christ through relationships: family, neighbours, colleagues, classmates, and friends. A conversation over tea, a whispered testimony at work, a midnight visit to pray for a sick relative - these are the primary means through which the gospel spreads.

In universities, believers meet one-on-one with seeking students. In factories, labourers gather quietly after shifts to read Scripture. In rural villages, evangelists travel from home to home, sometimes walking for hours, sometimes riding motorbikes through difficult terrain.

Healing and deliverance often open doors for the gospel. Many testimonies describe moments when believers prayed for the sick and God intervened. These encounters foster curiosity and openness. In areas where traditional folk religion or ancestor veneration remains strong, Christians often minister to those oppressed by fear or spiritual bondage. Evangelism does not diminish under persecution - it intensifies. Believers recognise that time may be short. Arrest could come unexpectedly. Therefore, they live with urgency. They share their faith boldly yet wisely, trusting God to guide their conversations.

Technology, surveillance, and the resilient church

China's rapid technological development has created both challenges and opportunities for the church. Surveillance cameras, facial-recognition software, and digital tracking make it increasingly difficult for believers to gather without detection. Messaging apps are monitored. Social media posts are always scrutinised. Phone calls may be recorded.

Yet the church has learned to adapt. Believers use encrypted apps, coded language, and offline communication. They change meeting locations frequently. They gather in small groups to stay under the radar. Pastors refrain from posting identifiable content online. Many young believers learn digital safety practices early, understanding that cyber-vigilance is now a key part of modern discipleship.

At the same time, technology has also become a tool for evangelism and discipleship. Online sermons, worship songs, digital Bibles, theological courses, and prayer networks circulate quietly through encrypted channels. Believers access global Christian teaching discreetly. Pastors receive encouragement from international brothers and sisters. Despite restrictions, the digital age has given the church unprecedented access to resources.

This paradox - surveillance on one side, spiritual connectivity on the other - creates a complex environment. Yet God works through both limitations and opportunities. As the Apostle Paul wrote from prison, *"God's word is not chained."* (2 Timothy 2:9).

A movement of courage and hope

The Chinese house-church movement stands as one of the most compelling testimonies of God's work in the world today. It reveals a church unshakeable in its devotion, courageous in suffering, and relentless in mission. It demonstrates that the gospel flourishes not because the environment is favourable but because Jesus is Lord.

Stories of transformation: The Gospel changes everything

The heart of China's house-church movement is not its structure, numbers, or resilience - it is its people. The real story of revival is always the story of transformed lives. Across China - rural villages, bustling cities, mountain towns, megacities, university campuses, factories, and remote ethnic regions - the gospel continues to reshape identities, restore families, heal wounds, and ignite courage in ordinary men and women.

In a rural province long known for its poverty and superstition, an entire village have now turned to Christ after witnessing the transformation of just one notoriously violent man. Alcoholism, gambling, and rage had dominated his life for decades. His family lived in fear. But one night, while lying sick in bed, he cried out to the God he had heard about from a neighbour. The following morning, something had changed. His anger was gone. His cravings vanished. He asked his family's forgiveness. Then he asked to learn about Jesus.

Weeks later, he was baptised in a river nearby. Soon after, dozens in his village became believers, saying, *"If God can change him, He can change anyone."* Today, the village hosts three thriving house churches.

In a major coastal city, a university student burdened by anxiety and academic pressure encountered Christ through an underground campus ministry. She had spent years striving for perfection, driven by her family's expectations. Anxiety attacks made her fear she would fail her studies. One evening, a Christian classmate invited her to a prayer gathering. There she heard the words of Jesus: *"Come to me, all you who are weary and burdened, and I will give you rest."* (Matthew 11:28). She wept uncontrollably. Within months, she became a quiet but passionate evangelist, leading Bible studies in dorm rooms and discipling other young women searching for peace.

In a police academy on the outskirts of a major city, a cadet secretly downloaded a digital Bible just out of curiosity. He had grown up hearing that Christianity was a Western threat, yet he found himself inexplicably drawn to the teachings of Jesus. The Sermon on the Mount captivated him. He read it every night, whispering the words in darkness. Over time, he committed his life to Christ. Despite enormous risk to his career, he became a quiet witness among colleagues, praying secretly with those who were troubled and sharing Scripture in discreet conversations. Years later, he would lead a small fellowship of public servants meeting in private homes - men and women who trusted him because he had first trusted Christ.

These stories are repeated countless times across China. The transformation is profound and unmistakable. Believers speak often of peace replacing fear, joy replacing despair, and courage replacing timidity. They describe the gospel of Christ not merely as doctrine but as liberation.

Prayer that sustains a movement

If there is one spiritual practice that defines the Chinese house-church movement, it is prayer. Prayer is not a ritual or a discipline – it's a lifeline. It's the hidden engine powering revival. It is woven into the rhythm of daily life.

Early-morning prayer meetings, midnight vigils, intercessory gatherings, fasting, prayer walks through neighbourhoods or fields - these are common across the nation.

Believers pray for protection, for the spread of the gospel, for imprisoned pastors, for wisdom under pressure, and for boldness to share Christ. They pray for neighbours, families, workplaces, and local authorities. They pray for reconciliation, for healing, for unity, and for renewed courage. In many house churches, prayer meetings last for hours, often in whispered tones, sometimes in tears, sometimes with overflowing joy.

Prayer sustains the movement when persecution intensifies. It strengthens believers when fear threatens to overwhelm. It joins scattered churches in spiritual unity. It keeps the focus on Christ rather than on circumstances. Many believers speak of miraculous answers to prayer - healings, protection during raids, timely warnings, and unexpected opportunities to share the gospel.

This emphasis on prayer echoes the early church described in Acts 1:14, where believers *"joined together constantly in prayer."* It also reflects the teaching of Jesus, who said, *"Always pray and not give up."* (Luke 18:1). The Chinese church has taken these words to heart, and God has honoured their perseverance.

The quiet power of house worship

In the absence of church buildings or public worship services, house-church music has taken on a unique character. Worship is often gentle, simple, and heartfelt. A small guitar, a keyboard, or even no instruments at all. Soft singing so neighbours won't hear. Songs that express devotion, longing, and courage. Many hymns were written by Chinese believers – many songs about perseverance, hope, trust, and the love of Christ in suffering. The lyrics often reflect themes of surrender:

- *"Even if the night is long, Your light is with me."*
- *"Take my fear and give me boldness."*
- *"Christ is enough for every trial."*
- *"The cross before me, the world behind me."*

Worship becomes a sanctuary in the midst of great pressure. It reminds believers that they are citizens of a greater kingdom. It binds hearts together. It lifts their eyes above oppression to the glory of Christ. Even children participate quietly. Families teach them to whisper Scripture songs, to pray simple prayers, and to trust Jesus. They grow up understanding that faith is precious and sometimes costly. Many of these children become bold witnesses in schools, universities, and workplaces later in life.

The rise of mission vision: China looks beyond its borders

One of the most remarkable developments in recent decades is the missionary vision emerging within the Chinese church. Despite facing domestic pressure, many believers sense that God is calling them to carry the gospel beyond China's borders - westward through Central Asia, the Middle East, and back toward Jerusalem. This vision is often associated with the *"Back to Jerusalem"* movement, not a formal organisation but an idea: that Chinese believers, shaped by suffering and perseverance, might take the gospel across regions resistant to Western missionaries. This vision is rooted in Scripture. Believers often cite the Great Commission, where Jesus commands His followers to *"go and make disciples of all nations."* (Matthew 28:19).

They also draw inspiration from the apostle Paul's missionary journeys. For many, this mission call is not theoretical - they prepare actively. Some learn whole new languages. Others study cultures. Some train in secret missionary schools. Many begin praying for specific nations.

What is striking is the willingness of believers to go even if they expect suffering abroad. Having endured hardship in China, they feel prepared to face it elsewhere. They see themselves not as victims but as ambassadors of Christ, carrying a message of hope, love, and salvation.

Challenges in a changing China

China today is changing very rapidly. Urbanisation, technology, political shifts, and cultural transitions all impact the church. Surveillance technology has made underground gatherings riskier. Legal restrictions have tightened. Some believers face social pressure from employers or educational institutions. Many pastors have been detained or questioned. Children and youth under eighteen face significant restrictions on participating in religious activities.

These challenges create real burdens. Some house churches have dissolved under pressure. Others have gone deeper underground. Leadership shortages are common, as many pastors face fatigue or long-term stress. The church's future will require resilience, wisdom, and dependence on God. Yet the believers remain hopeful. They look to Scripture, where God has repeatedly sustained His people through oppression, exile, and hardship. They remember the words of Jesus: *"I will not leave you as orphans; I will come to you."* (John 14:18). They trust that He will guide them through every challenge.

Hope for the Future

Despite outward pressures, the future of China's house-church movement is bright with spiritual hope. Young believers are rising with passion for the gospel. Urban professionals bring creativity and resources.

Rural churches bring depth of faith and perseverance. Digital tools enable believers to connect and disciple one another discreetly. Christian parents teach their children the stories of Scripture. Retired believers pray with quiet strength. Pastors shepherd their flocks with courage. Revival in China has never depended on favourable circumstances. It has always depended on God. And He remains faithful.

China's revival and the global church

The growth of the Chinese house-church movement is not an isolated regional phenomenon. Its influence extends far beyond China's borders, shaping global Christianity in surprising and profound ways. China's story is a vital chapter in the broader narrative of what God is doing throughout the world today.

As the second largest nation on earth by population, with a history of deep suffering and remarkable endurance, China now stands as a spiritual giant whose quiet faith is teaching the global church about perseverance, prayer, sacrifice, and mission.

One of the most significant contributions China brings to global Christianity is a renewed vision of discipleship. In many Western contexts today, discipleship has often become programmatic - anchored in classes, curricula, and scheduled events. In China, discipleship is life-on-life, relational, costly, and urgent. It flows through shared meals, late-night conversations, whispered prayers, and Scripture reading. It is forged in persecution, refined by hardship, and strengthened in community.

Across the world, pastors and mission leaders study the Chinese house-church model for its resilience, adaptability, and depth. They observe how believers multiply quickly, how small groups remain flexible, and how discipleship thrives under pressure. These insights have influenced mission strategies in Africa, the Middle East, South Asia, and Latin America - regions where restrictions and persecution are also increasing. In this way, China is quietly teaching the worldwide church how to thrive without relying on public platforms, institutional security or large gatherings.

It is reminding believers everywhere that the heart of the church is not a physical structure but the gathered people of God who carry His presence wherever they go.

The church in China as a mirror to the west

China's revival is also serving as a spiritual mirror for Western Christianity. For decades, many Western churches have enjoyed religious freedom, financial stability, and cultural acceptance. Yet in recent years, Western nations have seen rising secularism, declining church attendance, and growing scepticism toward Christianity. In this context, the Chinese church offers a counter-narrative: a vibrant, growing movement flourishing without the external privileges that many Western believers take for granted.

This contrast challenges the global church to examine what truly sustains faith. China's revival has not relied on favourable laws, social prestige, or elaborate programmes. It has thrived on Scripture, prayer, community, and courageous obedience. Believers have grown strong because they know their faith may cost them everything. Their devotion is not casual; it is total.

Western churches, confronted with cultural pressures of their own, are increasingly looking to China for inspiration. They see in Chinese believers a model of spiritual discipline, biblical devotion, and sacrificial love. China's testimony encourages Western Christians to rediscover the core of the gospel, to embrace simplicity, and to cultivate resilience in a changing cultural landscape.

China: A force in global evangelisation

Perhaps the most far-reaching impact of China's revival is its growing role in global evangelisation. Despite restrictions at home, Chinese believers possess a deep missionary instinct. They see themselves as part of God's redemptive story not only within China but across the nations. The vision known as *"Back to Jerusalem"* has stirred thousands of believers to pray for the unreached peoples stretching westward from China through Central Asia, the Middle East, and North Africa.

This missionary impulse is not driven by romanticism or triumphalism - it is birthed in prayer, sacrifice, and obedience. Many who feel called to go know they may face hardship or persecution abroad, just as they have at home. Yet they go with joy, trusting that the same God who sustained them in China will sustain them wherever He leads.

Already, Chinese believers are quietly serving in countries across Asia, Africa, and the Middle East. They work as teachers, business workers, engineers, students, or labourers while sharing Christ in culturally sensitive ways. Their background often gives them unique access - less likely to be viewed through the lens of Western politics, and more able to blend into local communities.

This missionary wave is still in its early stages, but its potential is enormous. If even a small percentage of China's millions of believers respond to the call of global mission, the impact on the unreached world will be unprecedented. The seeds of this future are already planted.

The role of suffering in global revival

China's experience has served to reshape the global church's understanding of suffering. In a world where hardship is often avoided or feared, Chinese believers demonstrate that suffering can be a catalyst for spiritual awakening. Their faithfulness under pressure has awakened global compassion, inspired prayer movements, and challenged complacency.

Stories of imprisoned pastors, persecuted believers, and resilient communities have drawn intercession from Christians around the world. Prayer networks span continents. churches in Africa, Europe, the Americas, and Oceania regularly pray for China's believers. In this way, the Chinese church has become a focal point for global unity in prayer.

Moreover, Chinese believers themselves pray fervently for the global church. They see their suffering not as a reason for self-pity but as a platform for intercession.

In prayer meetings across China, believers lift up nations they have never visited, missionaries they have never met, and churches they have never seen. They pray for revival in the West, for strength in Africa, for perseverance in the Middle East, for courage in South Asia, and for unity in Christ's body worldwide. Their prayer reveals a profound truth: revival is never local. It is global. What God does in one nation has global ripple effects.

China's contribution to global ecclesiology

China's church also offers a model of unity across diversity. House-churches come in many forms - rural networks, urban professional fellowships, family gatherings, migrant worker churches, ethnic minority communities, and various student movements.

They differ in worship style, in their leadership structure, and in theological emphasis. Some lean charismatic, others are more traditional. Some prioritise evangelism, others focus more on discipleship or social care.

Yet despite these differences, Chinese believers are bound by a deep sense of spiritual unity. They see themselves as one body and the family of Christ in China. This unity is not achieved through formal institutions or denominational structures. It arises from shared suffering, shared mission, shared prayer, and shared love for Jesus. This unity stands in stark contrast to the fragmentation often seen in Western Christianity.

The global church is learning from China what it means to maintain unity in diversity - to hold different expressions of worship, leadership, and theology together under the Lordship of Christ, recognising that persecution purifies and bonds more effectively than programmes ever could.

China's future: Between pressure and promise

As China looks toward the future, the church faces a number of uncertainties. Political pressure may intensify. Surveillance may increase. Restrictions may tighten. Leaders may face some new challenges. And yet, believers remain hopeful.

They trust the God who carried them through the darkest decades of the twentieth century. They trust the Christ who promised, *"Surely I am with you always, to the very end of the age."* (Matthew 28:20). They trust the Spirit who continues to move in power through small gatherings, whispered prayers, and courageous witness.

The future of China's revival will not depend on favourable circumstances but on the unchanging faithfulness of God. And He is at work still.

5. AFRICA ON FIRE: REVIVAL, RENEWAL, AND THE RISE OF THE GLOBAL SOUTH

Africa today stands as one of the most spiritually vibrant regions in the world. What was once viewed by Western missionaries as a land to be reached has now become one of the most dynamic epicentres of Christian renewal. The continent's story is not one of a single revival event or a single country's awakening, but a sweeping, continent-wide movement characterised by prayer, worship, evangelism, and remarkable resilience in the face of hardship. Africa is not merely experiencing periodic renewal — it is in the midst of a generational transformation reshaping global Christianity.

This chapter traces the unprecedented continent-wide rise of a Spirit-empowered, deeply rooted Christian movement, looking at how and why Africa has become such fertile soil for spiritual awakening, and how the church there has matured into one of the most influential forces in the global South.

A continent prepared by history, hardship, and hope

Africa's present renewal cannot be understood apart from its unique historical journey. The twentieth century brought some profound upheavals - colonialism, political revolutions, ethnic conflict, economic instability, and social fragmentation. Yet, through these storms, a remarkable spiritual hunger was born. African theologians often note that Christianity took deep root in Africa not because it was imported, but because it resonated with African worldviews: spiritual reality is taken seriously; prayer is natural; community is central; worship is expressive; suffering is understood not as defeat, but as an arena in which God acts.

In many places, Christianity spread not through institutions but through ordinary believers - farmers, teachers, traders, mothers, youth, migrants - whose resilient faith grew stronger under pressure. Persecution in some regions purified and strengthened communities; hardship drove believers deeper into prayer; instability created openness to spiritual hope.

As one Nigerian pastor famously said, *"When everything around us shakes, Christ becomes the only Rock."* Unlike other continents where modernity has often diminished spiritual hunger, Africa moved in the opposite direction: hardship intensified the longing for God, and revival met that longing.

Prayer movements that sustain transformation

Across the continent, prayer is the engine of renewal. But unlike earlier Western movements that emphasised scheduled prayer gatherings, African prayer movements are marked by intensity, longevity, and communal depth. Early-morning prayer walks, overnight vigils, multi-day prayer gatherings, multiple outdoor intercession meetings, and churchwide fasts are woven into the spiritual life of many African congregations.

These are not events which are appended to church programs, they *are* the heartbeat of the church. In nations experiencing political tension or economic struggle, prayer gatherings often fill entire nights, with believers interceding for protection, peace, national leaders, and the advance of the gospel.

African believers take passages like 1 Thessalonians 5:17, *"pray continually"* and *"call on me in the day of trouble."* (Psalm 50:15) with profound seriousness. The result is a culture in which prayer is not a discipline for the spiritually mature but the natural reflex of the community. This prayer-driven culture has shaped the continent's spiritual DNA, preparing the soil for revival in ways that programmes, strategies, or imported methods never could.

Worship as a cultural and spiritual force

If prayer is the engine of African revival, then worship is its oxygen. African worship is not merely musical expression - it is communal formation. It bridges generations, languages, and ethnic groups. Whether accompanied by drums in a rural village or electronic instruments in a sprawling urban megachurch, worship across Africa is marked by:

- Uninhibited joy and movement
- Call-and-response participation
- Testimonies woven into services
- Songs that reflect Scripture, struggle, and hope
- Congregational ownership rather than performance

The Psalms come alive in African worship: *"Shout for joy to the Lord, all the earth."* (Psalm 100:1) is not an instruction but an instinct. Worship becomes a safe space where the community can process its pain, expresses gratitude, proclaims hope, and encounters the presence of God. Many testimonies of healing, deliverance, and restoration occur during extended times of worship rather than formal ministry. This worship culture is one reason the African church remains resilient: people are not spectators but participants; worship does not entertain, it strengthens.

Evangelism that flows through everyday life

Africa's explosive Christian growth - from roughly 9% Christian in 1900 to well over 50% today - did not occur primarily through crusades, conferences, or mass media. Rather, the gospel spread through relationships, testimony, local leaders, and grassroots movement. Much of African evangelism happens in:

- University campuses
- Market stalls
- Rural farming communities
- Mining camps
- Refugee settlements
- Public transport hubs
- Workplaces and schoolrooms

Believers share Christ simply because they cannot keep silent about what God has done. Testimonies of answered prayer, deliverance, healing, or protection influence neighbours and family members more effectively than formal apologetics.

The Acts 1:8 vision - being witnesses *"to the ends of the earth."* - is embodied in daily life. Crucially, evangelism is not viewed as a specialist calling for a trained few, but a natural expectation for every believer. This is why African Christianity grows through networks rather than through systems, through movement rather than machinery.

Resilience in the face of opposition

Africa's revival story includes chapters of persecution, violence, and spiritual conflict. In regions of North and East Africa, many believers face severe pressure from various extremist groups or restrictive governments. churches are burned, pastors arrested, believers threatened. Yet the revival persists.

In some countries, the fastest church growth occurs in the most dangerous regions. Believers gather secretly, worship quietly, and share Scripture discreetly - and the fire spreads. This mirrors the early church, where opposition sharpened witness rather than silenced it. As Paul wrote, *"we are more than conquerors through him who loved us."* (Romans 8:37), and African believers have taken that to heart.

This resilience is not fuelled by bravado but by deep spirituality. African Christians know suffering is part of following Christ; they read stories of persecution in Acts not as history but as lived experience.

A maturing faith shaping the continent

One really encouraging developments in African Christianity is its maturity. The continent is no longer experiencing *conversion growth* alone but discipleship growth. churches are investing in Bible training, leadership development, theological education, and social impact initiatives. African scholars, theologians, and pastors are shaping Christian thought globally.

Pentecostal, evangelical, Anglican, Catholic, and independent churches - diverse in style but united in Christ - are partnering for mission, training leaders, and confronting issues such as corruption, tribal conflict, and poverty.

Moreover, African Christianity is increasingly self-sustaining. churches plant churches. Networks form organically. Funding often comes from within communities rather than from foreign supporters. The movement is becoming not only large but strong.

Africa as a mission-sending continent

The most surprising outcome of this great African renewal is that Africa has become a mission force. Nigerian, Kenyan, Ghanaian, Ugandan, and Ethiopian missionaries serve across Europe, Asia, the Middle East, and even across the Americas. African diaspora communities plant churches in cities like London, Amsterdam, Toronto, Sydney, and Seoul.

This is not a return of Western missions - it is a reversal. The Great Commission flows in every direction, fulfilling the biblical vision that *"all nations"* will both receive *and* proclaim the gospel. Africa's missionaries bring prayer, perseverance joy, worship, and spiritual authority - gifts shaped through decades of revival.

The continent where prayer shapes public life

Across Africa, prayer is not merely a private devotion but a shaping force that influences families, communities, workplaces, and nations. In many countries, dawn prayer is normal, not the exception. Offices, schools, transport hubs, and government facilities may begin the day with brief moments of Scripture and prayer. Taxi drivers pray before starting their shifts. Market traders gather to ask God's blessing on the day's trade. Villages hold weekly all-night vigils that stretch until sunrise.

This embedded culture of prayer predates the modern revival waves but has intensified dramatically in the past two decades. In Nigeria, Ghana, Uganda, Kenya, Ethiopia, and Rwanda, annual prayer gatherings attract tens of thousands - and in some cases, hundreds of thousands - of believers. These are not entertainment-driven events but earnest assemblies seeking God's presence and intervention in national issues such as corruption, violence, economic strain, and family challenges.

The effect is spiritual resilience. Prayer has become the reflex of the continent. Rather than withdrawing in fear amid conflict, poverty, or instability, believers press into intercession. They do not see prayer as an escape from reality but as the place where they gain strength to confront reality. Jesus' counsel -*"Always pray and not give up."* (Luke 18:1) - is not an abstract ideal in Africa. It is lived theology. Prayer is the furnace that keeps revival alive, the unbroken rhythm behind church growth and spiritual renewal.

A holistic gospel reaching the margins

One of the defining features of Africa's present transformation is the holistic character of the gospel being lived out. African revival is not limited to personal salvation or emotional renewal - it touches physical needs, social structures, and community relationships.

churches across the continent are now pioneering ministries in education, medical care, food distribution, addiction recovery, literacy, agriculture development, and reconciliation work. These ministries are not Western imports; they are grassroots initiatives responding to real needs in the community. Many pastors and evangelists are now bi-vocational, serving both as spiritual shepherds and community developers. This practical expression of faith reflects the biblical vision of a gospel that restores the whole person:

- Jesus healed bodies
- Jesus restored dignity
- Jesus fed the hungry
- Jesus defended the poor
- Jesus reconciled enemies
- Jesus proclaimed the Kingdom

African believers instinctively connect spiritual renewal with social transformation. They see no contradiction between preaching and planting maize, between praying and building a school, between worship and launching a clinic.

One pastor in rural Kenya described it simply: *"We preach salvation, and we grow food. The people need both."* This holistic gospel has a magnetic quality. Non-Christians often encounter the church first not through a sermon but through the kindness of believers who help with a medical bill, repair a roof, or teach a child to read. These everyday acts of grace open doors for conversations about Christ.

church planting and evangelism at scale

Africa's population is growing rapidly, and the church is growing even faster. What is striking is not only the scale but the diversity of evangelistic methods across the continent. In major cities, gospel initiatives take place through university ministries, professional networks, business fellowships, and contemporary worship gatherings that draw thousands of young adults. In rural regions, evangelists move from village to village on foot or motorbike, carrying Bibles, portable speakers, and a deep burden for unreached communities.

church planting is organic but intentional. In Uganda, one ministry plants churches by discipling a handful of households in a village first, then hosting open-air Bible discussions, then forming a worshipping community once there is local interest. In Zambia, evangelists partner with the local farmers to establish discipleship groups that meet after harvest, turning agricultural seasons into spiritual seasons. In northern Nigeria and the Horn of Africa, outreach is carried out quietly and courageously among communities where Christian belief is costly.

The Book of Acts is never far from the surface. When believers hear Paul's words - *"I have become all things to all people so that by all possible means I might save some."* (1 Corinthians 9:22) - they hear their own calling. As a result, thousands of congregations have been birthed in the past decade. Some are large urban churches with multiple services. Others meet under a tree or in a schoolroom. Many worship in temporary structures built from timber and iron sheeting while waiting for resources to construct permanent buildings. What they share is a sense of purpose: the gospel must be proclaimed, and disciples must be formed.

Renewal of worship and a deep love for Scripture

Worship across Africa is vibrant, communal, and expectant. It is characterised by sincerity rather than style, though styles differ from region to region. In West Africa, drums, harmonies, and call-and-response energise praise. In East Africa, worship is often dance-filled, joyful, and vocally expressive. In Southern Africa, choral traditions merge with contemporary worship to create unique sounds that have travelled globally. Ethiopian congregations draw on ancient liturgical traditions rooted in early Christianity.

But beyond the sound is the substance: African worship overflows with gratitude, hope, spiritual hunger, and keen awareness of God's nearness. Many services include extended periods of spontaneous prayer and singing. Testimonies are regular because believers want others to know what the Lord has done for them.

Worship is also deeply connected to Scripture. The Bible is cherished, read publicly, quoted frequently, memorised extensively, and applied to daily life. Believers do not merely admire Scripture - they rely on it. When Jesus declared, *"Your word is truth."* (John 17:17), His words became an anchor for African Christians navigating complicated realities.

In many regions, new believers receive their first Bible with reverence. Some churches run literacy programmes specifically so new Christians can read Scripture for themselves. The combination of worship and Word creates mature disciples whose faith does not evaporate under pressure.

The role of local communities and family networks

Unlike some Western contexts where faith has become highly individualistic, African revival remains deeply communal. churches function as extended families - places of support, accountability, celebration, correction, and belonging. When someone is sick, the church visits. When someone loses a job, others contribute.

When a young couple marries, the congregation gathers in support. When someone comes to Christ, their whole family often explores the faith together. This community ethos is one reason revival spreads so effectively. When one household is transformed, the relational web surrounding them becomes fertile ground for the gospel. A single conversion may influence dozens of relatives, neighbours, and friends. In this sense, revival moves along relational lines rather than organisational lines.

This mirrors the pattern seen in Scripture: Cornelius's household (Acts 10), Lydia's household (Acts 16), and the Philippian jailer's family (Acts 16). Africa's revival is happening not just in church buildings but in kitchens, courtyards, living rooms, fields, and marketplaces.

Persecution and perseverance

In several African nations, following Jesus comes with danger. Believers face intimidation, social exclusion, property loss, or violence. Yet the church grows. Many who live in hostile regions describe their persecution not as a deterrent but as a purifier. It strengthens resolve, deepens prayer, and intensifies love within the fellowship.

These believers often quote Jesus' words: *"In this world you will have trouble. But take heart! I have overcome the world."* (John 16:33) Their courage is not born of naivety but of conviction that Christ is worth everything.

And this courage, seen across the continent, is inspiring other nations. African intercessors pray passionately for persecuted believers in Asia and the Middle East. African missionaries willingly go into difficult regions. African pastors teach global audiences about endurance and faith under pressure.

A sending continent: Africa's missionary expansion

One of the most remarkable developments of recent decades is the shift from Africa being primarily *a mission field* to becoming *a mission force*. This transformation is not symbolic - it is actually measurable, strategic, and spiritually potent.

In countries such as Nigeria, Kenya, Ghana, Uganda, Ethiopia, and South Africa, churches are commissioning and sending missionaries to regions historically considered difficult mission contexts: North Africa, the Sahel, Central Asia, the Middle East, Europe, and increasingly hard secularised Western nations.

African missionaries often bring advantages that Western missionaries cannot. They understand life under pressure. They know how to pray through adversity. They are accustomed to spiritual warfare and have experience ministering in contexts of poverty, instability, and pluralistic religion. Many of the people speak multiple languages and can adapt easily to new cultural environments. Their theological training, increasingly provided through indigenous institutions, is grounded in Scripture, prayer, and practical ministry.

This missionary wave reflects a profound biblical pattern. The church at Antioch - diverse, prayerful, and Spirit-led - sent out workers into the Roman world (Acts 13:1-3). In similar fashion, African churches today are laying hands on men and women, commissioning them to carry the gospel into regions resistant to Western influence. It is a quiet but powerful turning of the tide. Where once missionaries arrived from Europe and North America, now missionaries depart from Lagos, Nairobi, Addis Ababa, and Kampala. The 'missionary DNA' of African Christianity is becoming one of the defining marks of global faith in the twenty-first century.

Holistic transformation: Revival that changes communities

Africa's revival is not limited to individual salvation experiences or dynamic worship gatherings. Across the continent, believers are integrating faith with social transformation, education, health, reconciliation, and economic empowerment. This holistic dimension reflects the biblical conviction that the gospel brings life to the whole person and the whole community. In many rural regions, churches run primary schools, literacy programs, microfinance initiatives, and agricultural training. Local congregations become centres of stability where government infrastructures may be fragile or absent.

Christian clinics provide essential medical care. Youth ministries address issues of unemployment, violence, and substance abuse. Prayer groups connect with local needs - feeding programs, safe houses for vulnerable children, and support for widows or refugees. This is revival with hands and feet.

Some African nations have seen entire districts transformed as the gospel takes root. Crime declines. Corruption decreases. Cooperation increases. Families stabilise. Education advances. Hope rises. Revival becomes visible not only in worship gatherings but in daily life. This pattern echoes Isaiah's vision: "Violence will no longer be heard in your land, nor ruin or destruction within your borders" (Isaiah 60:18). It is a foretaste of the kingdom breaking into earthly realities. African Christians do not separate personal salvation from social transformation; they see them as complementary expressions of Christ's reign.

When worship shapes society

A striking characteristic of African revival is the way worship spills out of the church buildings into public spaces. Worship gatherings often transition into community prayer marches, open-air singing, and dynamic evangelistic concerts that attract thousands. In regions such as West Africa, late-night worship services sometimes continue into the early hours of the morning, with entire neighbourhoods hearing the singing and prayer.

This public worship culture is not superficial exuberance - it is rooted in spiritual reality. Many African believers describe worship as warfare, healing, and proclamation combined. When they sing, they believe darkness is pushed back and strongholds are broken. When they dance, they celebrate the freedom Christ has given them. When they pray aloud, they believe chains of oppression are shattered.

This has shaped national identity. In some countries, Christian holidays become public festivals filled with music and prayer. Camp meetings attract tens of thousands. Youth choirs fill city squares. Gospel music permeates the culture through radio, television, and social media. Worship becomes a cultural force.

The Western church, often subdued in its expression, finds in African worship a reminder of David's declaration: *"I will celebrate before the Lord."* (2 Samuel 6:21). Africa's revival shows that exuberant worship and deep theology are not opposites, they are companions.

The church as a healing community

Across Africa, churches have become havens for healing - emotional, relational, and spiritual. Many communities bear the scars of civil war, ethnic conflict, political persecution, famine, or natural disasters. In such contexts, the church plays a prophetic and pastoral role, offering reconciliation ministries, trauma counselling, prayer for deliverance, and practical support.

Believers gather to pray over victims of violence, to support widows and orphans, and to mediate reconciliation between fractured groups. Pastors often serve as informal counsellors, peace-brokers, and community leaders.

In post-conflict zones such as Rwanda, parts of Uganda, South Sudan, and Sierra Leone, churches have led reconciliation initiatives that have brought deep healing where government programs struggled to penetrate.

This healing dimension reflects the ministry of Jesus, who proclaimed both forgiveness and freedom. *"He has sent me to bind up the broken-hearted."* (Isaiah 61:1). African churches take this call seriously. They create spaces where the broken find hope and where the oppressed find release.

The crucial role of theological depth

One of the challenges facing rapid-growing churches worldwide is the danger of shallow discipleship. African leaders have recognised this and responded intentionally. Right across the continent, theological education is expanding rapidly, not through Western institutions, but through African-led Bible colleges, seminaries, digital platforms, and many church-based training schools.

A new generation of African theologians is emerging - men and women writing from within their cultural context, addressing African questions with biblical clarity.

They tackle many issues such as prosperity theology, spiritual syncretism, ancestor veneration, tribal conflict, and the interface between traditional religion and Christianity. Their work strengthens the church's foundation.

This theological maturity ensures long-term stability for revival. Rapid growth becomes sustainable growth. Worship is anchored in truth. Prayer is shaped by Scripture. Mission is fuelled by a sound gospel. Africa's renewal is not simply emotional or experiential - it is increasingly theologically robust.

The future: Africa and the next wave of global Christianity

As the twenty-first century progresses, demographic projections show Africa becoming the epicentre of global Christianity. By 2050, more than half of all Christians worldwide will live on the African continent. This demographic shift will have profound implications for mission, theology, global Christian leadership and worship.

Africa stands at a pivotal moment. The church is young, vibrant, and multiplying. It is steadily maturing theologically. It is increasingly engaged in global mission. It is investing in education, technology, and leadership development. It is shaping the next wave of Christian scholarship, worship, and spiritual formation.

If current trends continue, Africa will play a defining role in global Christianity for generations. The centre of gravity for world evangelisation will shift decisively southward. The rhythms of African worship, the depth of African prayer, the courage of African believers, and the insight of African theologians will shape the future of the church.

This is not a regional revival. It is a continental awakening with global significance.

A continent that teaches the world to pray, worship, and believe again

Africa's revival reminds the global church of essential truths:

- God moves powerfully among the humble.
- Prayer is the engine of renewal.
- Worship is warfare.
- Mission belongs to every believer.
- Holistic transformation is part of the gospel.
- Indigenous leadership is God's long-term strategy.
- Revival is not confined to one culture, nation, or hemisphere.

In a world so troubled by anxiety, division, and secularism, the African church stands as a signpost: God is not done. God is moving. God is building His church in places where many least expected it.

Africa is not only on fire - it is lighting torches that will carry the gospel well into the twenty-first century and beyond.

6. LATIN AMERICA'S TRANSFORMATION: THE CHARISMATIC WAVE

Across the vast expanse of Latin America - stretching from the bustling barrios of Mexico City to the Amazon rainforest, from the Andean highlands to the mega-cities of Brazil - an extraordinary spiritual movement has transformed the religious landscape over the last several decades. This movement is commonly described as the *Charismatic Wave*. It is marked by passionate worship, prayer for healing, prophetic ministry, evangelistic zeal, and a hunger for the presence and power of the Holy Spirit. It is one of the most significant spiritual awakenings of the modern era.

While Latin America was historically shaped by Catholicism - often traditional, institutional, and culturally inherited - the past fifty years have seen a dramatic shift. Tens of millions have come to embrace a living, personal faith in Jesus Christ. Churches of all denominations have been renewed. Worship has become vibrant, participatory, and expectant. Prayer movements have multiplied. Entire communities have been transformed. The Holy Spirit has breathed fresh life into the region.

The story of Latin America's charismatic renewal is not confined to one country or one denomination. It is a continental movement, sweeping through major urban centres, small rural towns, indigenous communities, and a variety of multicultural environments. It is marked by social transformation, spiritual hunger, and a rediscovery of the dynamic power of the New Testament church. This chapter explores that story - beginning with Brazil, the epicentre of the modern wave, and then moving through the broader transformation shaping the continent today.

Brazil: The beating heart of the Charismatic Wave

Any exploration of Latin America's transformation must begin with Brazil. Home to more than 200 million people, Brazil has experienced one of the most dramatic religious shifts in the world.

Once overwhelmingly Catholic, the nation has seen explosive growth among Pentecostal and Charismatic believers. Today, more than one-third of all Brazilians identify as evangelical or charismatic. Much of this growth has come through local, indigenous, Spirit-filled churches that all emphasise prayer, worship, healing, deliverance, and community.

Brazilian Christianity is deeply expressive - marked by joyful singing, spontaneous prayer, dancing, tears of repentance, testimonies of transformed lives, and fervent preaching of the gospel. Services can last hours. Prayer meetings often spill into the early morning. Worship gatherings fill stadiums. Prayer walks move through entire neighbourhoods. The believers frequently fast, intercede, and gather in small groups throughout the week. The spiritual atmosphere is alive with expectancy.

Many factors contribute to this growth. One is the preaching of Jesus as a living, present Saviour who heals, restores, forgives, and empowers. There's also a strong emphasis on community. Churches provide support for the poor, the struggling, the addicted, and the marginalised. A third factor is the courage of ordinary believers who share their faith boldly, often through personal testimonies. In a society shaped by social inequality, many people are turning to Christ for hope, identity, and renewal.

Underneath the outward vibrancy is a deep theological foundation: a belief in the power of the Holy Spirit, the authority of Scripture, and the continued relevance of spiritual gifts. For many, the Book of Acts is not ancient history - it is a model of what God is doing now.

This movement is not dependent on a few large churches; it is woven into the fabric of everyday life. In São Paulo, Rio de Janeiro, Manaus, Recife, and right across rural Brazil, small congregations flourish in converted warehouses, temporary tents, open fields, and crowded living rooms. In the Amazon region, rivers become highways for missionaries travelling to remote communities. Indigenous Christians translate Scripture into local languages and plant churches along riverbanks.

In the favelas (slums), the believers form prayer circles, lead outreach programs, and care for children and families at risk. This is revival - raw, local, dynamic.

Spiritual hunger and the cry for renewal

Latin America's charismatic transformation did not arise in a vacuum. It has emerged from decades of social upheaval, poverty, political instability, dictatorship, corruption, and moral brokenness. Many communities suffered violence, addiction, family breakdown, and hopelessness. Into this vacuum, the gospel of Christ has entered with power - bringing healing, identity, forgiveness, and restoration.

A pattern is evident: the greater the need, the greater the openness to God. In neighbourhoods scarred by violence, churches have become safe havens. In communities torn by addiction, believers have become counsellors and mentors. In regions marked by spiritual oppression, worship has become liberation. People come seeking help - and they encounter Jesus.

This spiritual hunger reflects the words of Jesus: *"Blessed are those who hunger and thirst for righteousness, for they will be filled."* (Matthew 5:6). Many Latin American believers speak of this verse as their testimony. They were hungry, and God filled them. They were thirsty, and He gave them living water. They were broken, and He healed them.

This cry for renewal birthed prayer movements across the continent. All-night prayer vigils – *vigílias* - became common. Believers gathered in stadiums, beaches, mountains, and city squares seeking the presence of God. Houses turned into prayer rooms. Schools, marketplaces, and public offices were touched by spontaneous prayer meetings. In the midst of economic and political turmoil, people found stability in Christ.

The Spirit's work has been unmistakable: conversions, restored families, repentance, healings, reconciliation, and new faith. The charismatic wave has turned millions from nominal religion to living discipleship.

Worship as a catalyst for revival

Worship plays a central role in Latin America's transformation. Across the continent, worship has become a catalyst for revival - uniting generations, crossing many cultural boundaries, and expressing the longing of hearts humbled before God.

Brazilian worship leaders such as Ana Paula Valadão and many others helped inspire new songs that swept across the continent, blending Scripture, prayer, and a deep hunger for God's presence. Their influence has shaped entire church communities, conferences, and prayer movements.

But worship in Latin America is not driven by celebrity - it is fundamentally communal. In the local congregations, everyone participates. Worship is usually a full-body, full-voice, full-heart experience. It includes clapping, dancing, lifting hands, kneeling, weeping, and testimonies of answered prayer.

It reflects David's invitation: *"Come, let us sing for joy to the Lord; let us shout aloud to the Rock of our salvation."* (Psalm 95:1). This atmosphere of worship has created a spiritual environment in which faith grows, repentance deepens, and the Holy Spirit moves freely.

The spread of the Charismatic Wave across the continent

Although Brazil remains a global centre, the charismatic wave has swept powerfully across other nations:

- *Colombia:* home to massive prayer movements combating violence.
- *Argentina:* birthplace of the 1980s–1990s revival that shaped global charismatic worship.
- *Guatemala:* where prayer, fasting, and evangelism led to dramatic social change.
- *Chile, Peru, and Bolivia:* experiencing steady charismatic growth, especially among young adults.
- *Mexico:* seeing renewal movements in both Catholic and Protestant communities.

The details of each nation will be explored in the next part - but here is the key truth: revival is not contained by borders. The Spirit moves from city to city, village to village, nation to nation - awakening people to Christ.

Latin America is experiencing not simply a church growth phenomenon but a continental reformation of the heart. The story of Latin America's spiritual transformation is far larger than any single nation. What began as scattered charismatic renewals in the mid-twentieth century has become a continental movement reshaping churches, culture, mission, and public life from Mexico to Patagonia.

We turn now to three specific nations whose spiritual trajectories clearly illustrate the full breadth and depth of this remarkable transformation: Colombia, Argentina, and Chile. Though unique in history and culture, each nation displays the fingerprints of the same Holy Spirit at work - awakening the church, renewing worship, empowering preaching, and drawing millions into a vibrant walk with Jesus.

Colombia: Revival amid turmoil, renewal amid trauma

Few countries in the world have experienced the combination of violence, instability, and spiritual hunger that Colombia endured during the late twentieth century. For decades, armed conflict, cartel violence, kidnappings, and political upheaval created an atmosphere of deep fear. Cities were marked by bombings, corruption, and instability. Yet in this very environment - where hope seemed scarce and the church often felt powerless - God sparked a remarkable renewal.

The most famous example emerged in Bogotá through what became known as the *G12 Movement*, launched by pastor César Castellanos in the early 1990s. After a personal encounter with God that deeply changed his life and ministry, Castellanos developed a model of small-group discipleship built around the idea of cell leadership in multiples of twelve - mirroring Jesus' investment in the first twelve disciples. This model emphasised intense discipleship, personal evangelism, accountability, and multiplication.

Within a few years, a single church became a network of tens of thousands of small groups. Thousands were baptised. Families were restored. Former gang members, addicts, and broken homes experienced healing. The movement soon spread internationally - reaching Brazil, Peru, Mexico, South Korea, and parts of Europe. While the G12 model has been debated and adapted in various forms, no one disputes that Colombia witnessed a massive spiritual awakening in a time of national darkness.

Revival in Colombia was never merely numerical. Churches right across the nation - Pentecostal, Baptist, Methodist, and independent charismatic congregations – all experienced a fresh outpouring of the Holy Spirit. Worship became more expressive; prayer gatherings grew rapidly; fasting movements emerged; evangelism exploded. Large stadium events brought together thousands in unified prayer for peace and healing across the nation.

This movement reshaped Colombia's spiritual identity. It demonstrated that when a nation is shaken, God often raises up a praying church who believe His promise: *"Call to me and I will answer you."* (Jeremiah 33:3). Colombia's revival emerged not in ease but in trauma - and this has become part of its power. The darker the night, the brighter the flame.

Argentina: The fire that fell on the grasslands

Argentina holds a special place in the history of Latin American revival because it became the cradle of one of the most influential charismatic waves of the twentieth century. While seeds of renewal were present earlier, the movement truly ignited in the 1980s and 1990s through a series of large evangelistic campaigns, prayer movements, and powerful outpourings of the Spirit.

One pivotal moment was the 1982 Buenos Aires revival, where pastor Omar Cabrera and a group of evangelists saw thousands respond to the gospel in mass meetings filled with repentance, miracles, and tears. Around the same time, the ministry of Carlos Annacondia exploded across the nation.

A businessman turned evangelist, Annacondia preached with unusual authority and simplicity. His crusades routinely attracted massive crowds—sometimes tens of thousands per night. Testimonies of healing, deliverance, and salvation became widespread. It was common for hardened criminals to break down in tears, surrendering their weapons at the altar.

Annacondia's bold proclamation - *"Cristo te ama!"* (*"Christ loves you!"*) - became a national cry of hope. The movement deepened in the 1990s through the ministries of Claudio Freidzon, whose stadium gatherings in Buenos Aires introduced a fresh emphasis on intimacy with the Holy Spirit. Influenced by the Toronto Blessing yet distinctly Argentine in flavour, these gatherings were marked by extended worship, prophetic ministry, and profound encounters with God's presence. The phrase *"Holy Spirit, come!"* became the heart-cry of a generation.

The revival spread to local churches, transforming worship styles, preaching, youth ministry, and missions. Traditional liturgies gave way to contemporary worship, testimonies, and extended prayer times. Churches planted churches. Pastors were trained and sent. Youth movements exploded with missionary zeal. Many refer to this era as the *"Argentine Fire"*- a movement still felt across South America today.

What is most striking about Argentina's revival is not merely the signs and wonders but the transformation in the nation's spiritual atmosphere. churches that once struggled to grow became vibrant. Interdenominational unity flourished. A strong prayer movement emerged, including all-night vigils and weekly gatherings dedicated to crying out for national renewal. This revival was not imported - it was deeply Argentine, rooted in the nation's own culture, worship, and longing for God.

Chile: Quiet strength and steady flame

Chile's contribution to the charismatic wave often receives less attention than Brazil or Argentina, yet its influence is substantial. Chile has one of the highest rates of evangelical growth in the Western Hemisphere, with charismatic renewal playing a major role in shaping its churches, communities, and missions.

Unlike some regions marked by chaotic expression, Chilean revival has tended to be steady, disciplined, and deeply rooted in Scripture.

The Pentecostal Methodist church, founded in the early twentieth century, laid the groundwork for what would become one of the largest indigenous evangelical movements in Latin America. Rural revivals frequently emerged through passionate preaching, testimonies, healing, and vibrant worship.

During the difficult years of political turmoil - especially under military rule - churches became havens of hope. Pastors risked their lives to protect the vulnerable. Prayer gatherings multiplied in homes and small halls throughout the country. As these believers sought God with fasting and intercession, many experienced a deepening of spiritual gifts, boldness, and compassion.

A feature of Chile's movement has been the empowerment of lay leaders. Ordinary believers such as farmers, teachers, students, and labourers, found themselves preaching, leading worship, visiting the sick, and planting small congregations. These house-church networks, though less globally publicised, have spread revival throughout rural communities, mining towns, fishing villages, and urban neighbourhoods.

Chile also developed a very strong missionary impulse. Today, Chilean missionaries serve in North Africa, the Middle East, Asia, and Europe - quietly but faithfully bringing the gospel where Western missionaries sometimes struggle to gain access.

This missionary zeal is fuelled by worship gatherings where believers pray passionately for the nations, trusting the promise that *"the earth will be filled with the knowledge of the glory of the Lord as the waters cover the sea."* (Habakkuk 2:14).

A unified wave: One Spirit, many expressions

Although Colombia, Argentina, and Chile differ in their history, culture, and expression, the very same spiritual themes have appeared repeatedly:

- Deep prayer movements
- Vibrant worship and heartfelt repentance
- Strong evangelistic zeal
- Healing, deliverance, and supernatural encounters
- Multiplying small groups and churches
- Rising indigenous leadership
- Mission sending, both local and global

This is the heart of the Latin American charismatic wave: a Spirit-empowered movement that transforms lives, reshapes nations, and reinvigorates the global church.

A continent carried by the Spirit

Across Latin America, the Charismatic and Pentecostal renewal has not merely reshaped churches - it has actually reshaped society, culture, identity, and mission in ways that few global movements have done.

The story of this transformation is not only about emotional worship, spiritual gifts, or congregational expansion. It is about a profound re-centring of Latin American Christianity around the active presence of the Holy Spirit, a renewed hunger for Scripture, a rediscovery of community, and a bold missionary impulse reaching far beyond the continent itself.

A faith that shapes the streets, not just the church

One really notable features of the Latin American Charismatic movement is its influence outside the church walls. Worship spills into city squares, neighbourhood parks, beaches, bus stations, and street corners. Evangelism is public, bold, and unapologetic.

Whether in Bogotá, São Paulo, Guatemala City, or Santiago, it is common to see believers praying for the sick in public, offering food to the poor, or preaching the gospel to passers-by. Latin America's revival is intensely incarnational - it does not wait for people to enter a building. It moves toward them.

In some countries, crime-ridden neighbourhoods have been transformed as local churches began prayer walks, offered rehabilitation programmes, provided food distribution, and planted house fellowships. Former gang members now serve as pastors. Once-violent communities have established youth centres, sports ministries, and Bible-study hubs. The Charismatic wave has brought a social conscience shaped by the compassion of Jesus, who said, *"Whatever you did for one of the least of these brothers and sisters of mine, you did for me."* (Matthew 25:40). This outward-looking faith has become one of the hallmarks of renewal across the continent.

Theological depth beneath the vibrancy

Critics sometimes assume that Charismatic movements lack theological grounding. In Latin America, the opposite is increasingly true. Over the past two decades, a growing number of pastors, theologians, and Bible teachers within Charismatic circles have committed themselves to deeper study of Scripture, training, and doctrinal maturity. This theological development has produced several important outcomes:

1. *A return to Scripture as authority*
   Latin American renewal movements consistently emphasise the authority of the Bible. Preaching is central. Testimony is paired with teaching. Emotional expression is anchored in biblical truth.

2. *A balanced pneumatology*
   While the gifts of the Spirit remain a defining feature, many churches have emphasised discernment, character, and holiness. Leaders increasingly teach that the Spirit's work is not merely power but also transformation: *"The fruit of the Spirit is love, joy, peace, forbearance..."* (Galatians 5:22).

3. *Discipleship, not just experience*
   churches now emphasise small-group discipleship, accountability, and pastoral mentoring. Spiritual gifts are encouraged, but within structures that cultivate maturity.

4. *Unity across denominations*
   A growing number of Catholic Charismatic communities collaborate with evangelical and Pentecostal networks. This ecumenical openness - rare in other parts of the world - reflects the Spirit's unifying work.

The movement is maturing. The early wildfire of spontaneous revival is now supported by deep roots in Scripture, theology, and pastoral formation.

The rise of indigenous leadership and local expressions

Another defining feature of Latin America's transformation is the rise of local, indigenous leadership. Unlike earlier periods of missionary dependence, today's revival is led from within - from pastors, evangelists, worship leaders, and Bible teachers shaped by Latin American culture, language, and lived experience. This is significant for several reasons:

- *Authenticity increases:* Worship, preaching, and discipleship resonate culturally.
- *Sustainability grows:* Local leaders remain, endure, and train others.
- *Creativity emerges:* New worship styles, local theologies, indigenous mission models, and contextualised ministries flourish.

Churches across Latin America do not simply imitate global models—they create their own. Their identity is rooted in Scripture, shaped by the Spirit, and expressed through the rich cultural tapestry of the continent.

Missions: Latin America goes to the nations

A remarkable and often overlooked dimension of Latin America's renewal is its global missionary explosion. Tens of thousands of Latin American missionaries now serve in Africa, Asia, Europe, the Middle East, Oceania, and North America. Latin American missionaries bring something unique to the global church:

- Resilience shaped by hardship
- Warmth and relational depth
- Boldness in evangelism
- A Spirit-saturated worldview
- A willingness to go to hard places

Brazil alone sends tens of thousands of missionaries to unreached peoples. Colombia has become a missionary training hub. Argentina's worship movement has impacted the global church for decades. Central American missionaries serve in rural Asia and North Africa.

Latin America is now one of the largest missionary forces in the world. The Charismatic wave did not create inward-focused churches; it created outward-moving ones. The continent that once received missionaries now sends them.

Revival among the young

The Charismatic movement has drawn millions of young people - students, musicians, creatives, urban professionals, and young families. Youth services often overflow with worship that lasts for hours. Many movements report that more than half their congregations are under 35. Young people are attracted because:

- The worship is passionate
- The community is authentic
- The mission is compelling
- The presence of God feels real
- Scripture is preached in practical, life-changing ways

This amazing generational renewal is so crucial for long-term transformation. In so many countries, the youth are the ones who are planting churches, leading prayer vigils, serving the poor, organising evangelistic gatherings, and leading worship movements. The future of Latin American Christianity is vibrant because its young people are not disengaged - they are leading.

Deliverance, healing, and signs of the Spirit

One cannot understand Latin America's Charismatic wave without recognising the prevalence of healing, deliverance, and spiritual breakthrough. These are not fringe experiences; they are central to the movement's identity.

In communities wrestling with poverty, trauma, addiction, fear, and generational brokenness, the power of the Spirit brings tangible freedom. Many testimonies describe physical healing, release from spiritual oppression, restoration of marriages, and deep emotional healing.

This also aligns with Jesus' ministry: *"He sent them out to proclaim the kingdom of God and to heal the sick."* (Luke 9:2). Latin America's revival takes these words seriously.

Yet the movement also increasingly emphasises discernment and pastoral care. Healing ministries now operate alongside counselling, discipleship, and intercessory prayer to ensure long-term spiritual growth.

Social impact: When the Spirit touches a nation

Revival in Latin America has had a visible social impact:

- Drug addicts restored
- Gang violence confronted
- Community reconciliation initiatives
- Micro-enterprise ministries in poor districts
- Food programs established
- Orphan and widow care expanded
- Domestic violence addressed
- Youth leadership developed

Churches have become important social centres, prayer centres, educational social centres, and community shelters.

This holistic transformation clearly reflects the heart of Jesus Christ, who proclaimed good news to the poor, freedom to the oppressed, and hope to the broken (Luke 4:18).

A continent prepared for greater things

Latin America's Charismatic Wave shows no sign of slowing. Its churches are multiplying. Its worship is influencing the world. Its missionaries are crossing oceans. Its young leaders are rising. And its theology is maturing.

The Spirit is moving - not in a moment but in a generation. The continent once called *"the sleeping giant of Christianity"* is now wide awake - praise God!

7. THE 24-7 PRAYER MOVEMENT: A GLOBAL FURNACE OF INTERCESSION

In an age marked by speed, distraction, and spiritual fatigue, an unexpected global movement has quietly risen - one built not on programmes or personalities, but on prayer.

It began with a handful of young people in a small English coastal town, meeting in a warehouse in 1999 simply to seek God without stopping. They had no idea that what they were starting would ignite a worldwide movement of continuous intercession that has since touched more than half the nations of the earth.

The 24-7 Prayer Movement has become a massive furnace of global intercession, a catalyst for mission, and one of the most transformative spiritual developments in 25 years.

Unlike many historic revivals that erupt suddenly and burn intensely before fading, this movement has grown steadily, organically, relationally, and sustainably. It has flourished across denominations, cultures, languages, and continents.

What began as one prayer room has multiplied into thousands. What started as a single spark in the UK has become a worldwide constellation of prayer rooms, houses of prayer, mission teams, urban ministries, and communities committed to worship, justice, and intercession.

At its core, the 24-7 Prayer Movement is driven by a simple conviction: that when God's people pray, God moves. This is not prayer dressed in formality or ritual, but prayer that is raw, persistent, expectant, Spirit-led, and rooted in Scripture.

It is prayer shaped by Jesus' words: *"Ask and it will be given to you; seek and you will find; knock and the door will be opened to you."* (Matthew 7:7). It is prayer that believes God still visits His people, still opens doors, still saves, still heals, still revives.

The birth of a global rhythm

The story began in late 1999 in Chichester, England, where a young community felt called to pray without ceasing - literally. They set up a simple room in a warehouse: plain walls, a few Bibles, some cushions, pens, markers, candles. Not elaborate at all. Just a space for God. They took turns praying in hour-long shifts, day and night. What began as a one-month experiment grew beyond all expectation.

People encountered God in the room at all hours. Some wept in repentance. Others worshipped in joy. Some wrote prayers, confessions, poems, or Scriptures on the walls. A sense of God's presence filled the space with unmistakable holiness. It felt, many said, like "Jacob's ladder" - a place where heaven touched earth.

Word spread. Within months, prayer rooms sprang up in Europe, Asia, North America, Africa, and Australia. Students launched round-the-clock prayer rooms on campuses. churches dedicated spare rooms, basements, and halls. Families turned garages or attics into prayer spaces. The movement leapt across languages and cultures not through marketing but through testimony. Something ancient yet fresh was stirring, and people could feel it.

The early 2000s became a wave of intercession unlike anything seen in recent history. It was not polished. It often felt chaotic. It was decidedly grassroots. But it was unmistakably God-centred. The movement grew because ordinary believers wanted to pray, to seek God's face, to rediscover intimacy and urgency in their relationship with Him.

The heart of the prayer room

Every 24-7 prayer room is unique - because every culture across the globe expresses worship differently. But the core elements are the same: a consecrated space, continuous prayer, and an expectation that God will meet His people. Some rooms are simple and quiet. Others are artistic and expressive.

Some are located in churches; others are hidden in difficult parts of cities, operating like spiritual embassies in places of darkness. What matters is not the décor but the dedication. Someone is always praying. Someone is always interceding. Someone is always worshipping. Day and night, night and day, a constant offering rises to God, echoing the imagery of incense ascending before His throne (Revelation 5:8).

Inside these rooms, time feels different. People often say they entered for an hour but stayed for three. Many describe encountering God in ways they never had before. Others speak of breakthrough - answered prayers, restored relationships, renewed callings.

The prayer rooms become catalysts for mission, evangelism, and justice. People leave with fresh conviction, healed hearts, renewed courage. Prayer fuels action. Action drives people back to prayer. The cycle repeats.

A movement without borders

Perhaps the most compelling element of the 24-7 Prayer Movement is its adaptability. It crosses denominational lines with unusual ease. Anglicans, Pentecostals, Baptists, Methodists, Presbyterians, independents, and Catholics have all hosted prayer rooms. It is not owned by one church or theological tradition. It is a shared well.

This flexibility has allowed the movement to take root in some of the most unlikely places. Prayer rooms have appeared in nightclubs, prisons, refugee camps, university dormitories, mountain villages, urban slums, and corporate office spaces after hours.

In Europe, it helped rekindle faith in post-Christian contexts. In Africa, it blended with the vibrant worship and intercession traditions already present. In Latin America, it linked prayer with street ministry and evangelism. In Asia, it resonated with cultures shaped by contemplation and perseverance.

Everywhere it goes, it seems to carry the same DNA: intimacy with God, persistence in prayer, creativity in expression, and a deep expectation of God's activity.

An answer to a global longing

At the turn of the twenty-first century, many believers sensed a spiritual hunger rising across nations. churches were full of programmes but thin in prayer. Many Christians were busy but spiritually weary. Worship had grown more musical but less contemplative. Discipleship had become crowded with activity but low in stillness.

The 24-7 Prayer Movement arrived as a gentle but powerful correction - a call back to first things. A call to sit at the feet of Jesus. A call to listen. To linger. To intercede. To worship without agenda. To rediscover the simplicity and power of prayer. In a noisy, accelerated world, prayer rooms became places of holy stillness.

In an anxious generation, they became sanctuaries of peace. In places where faith was declining, they became seeds of renewal. In spiritually dark regions, they became outposts of light. This was not just a movement of activity - it was a movement of presence. A longing for God Himself.

Prayer leading to mission

From its earliest days, the movement insisted that prayer must fuel mission. Intercession without action risks becoming introspective. Action without prayer risks becoming shallow. The 24-7 Prayer Movement helped restore the biblical marriage of the two.

In the Book of Acts, prayer precedes mission. The Spirit falls when believers pray in unity. Missionaries are sent out after the church prays. Miracles follow prayer. Doors open through prayer. The gospel advances because God's people seek Him earnestly. The same dynamic has emerged in this movement.

Many new ministries were established - street evangelism teams, justice initiatives, youth outreaches, church plants, compassion projects, and cross-cultural mission teams — were birthed in the quiet of prayer rooms. People encountered God, heard His voice, and sensed His call. Prayer birthed mission. Mission drove believers back to prayer. And the cycle continues.

A movement marked by creativity, courage, and simplicity

One of the most remarkable features of the global 24-7 Prayer movement is the extraordinary creativity it has unleashed in the global church. Wherever prayer begins to flow freely without interruption - whether in a repurposed classroom, a renovated warehouse, a garage, a cabin, or a corner of a cathedral - worship becomes inventive and prayer becomes bold. The movement has demonstrated that when God's people are freed from program-driven structures and invited simply to pray, extraordinary things happen.

Prayer rooms are intentionally kept simple — often just four white walls, perhaps a cross, some art materials, markers, prayer stations, Bibles, a guitar, cushions on the floor, or maps of the world. The simplicity fosters focus. The lack of formality encourages freedom. Many describe these spaces not as places to "attend" prayer but as places to really *enter into* God's presence. Creativity explodes because prayer becomes participatory. People write prayers on the walls, they draw pictures, pin photographs of loved ones they are praying for, place Scriptures on the floor, or create stations that draw attention to specific injustices or nations. In youth groups, teenagers often fill walls with confessions, intercessions, and declarations of faith.

In university settings, students pray for their campus, professors, and friends by name. In urban centres, teams pray for human trafficking victims, refugees, the homeless, government leaders, and unreached people groups. young people who had never stayed awake through a prayer meeting suddenly found themselves praying through the night — burdened, joyful, wide-awake, and full of the Spirit. Many wept for their generation, repented of apathy, and interceded for their nations.

A prayer movement rooted in mission

From the beginning, this movement has carried a missionary heartbeat. It was never intended to create holy enclaves or contemplative retreats for their own sake. Instead, the model is simple: prayer fuels mission. A furnace of intercession generates outward movement into the world.

In countless stories, people emerge from a prayer room with a renewed sense of calling - to evangelism, social justice, church planting, or cross-cultural mission. Some are led to reconcile broken relationships. Others sense God calling them to serve the poor, care for the marginalised, or advocate for the oppressed. Many speak of hearing God's voice clearly for the first time - a whisper of direction, conviction, or encouragement that reshapes their lives.

Historically, this echoes the pattern that is found in the Bible. The church in Antioch fasted and prayed before the Holy Spirit commissioned Paul and Barnabas: *"Set apart for me Barnabas and Saul for the work to which I have called them."* (Acts 13:2). Mission flowed out of prayer. The 24-7 Prayer movement mirrors that rhythm. Intercession leads to action. Worship leads to witness. Listening to God leads to obedience.

Across Africa, Europe, Asia, Oceania, and the Americas, 24-7 prayer communities have engaged in missional outreach to refugees, migrants, the homeless, addicts, and victims of trafficking. Many host "boiler rooms" — small communities built around rhythms of prayer, hospitality, justice, and mission. The movement is not only praying around the clock; it is serving around the clock.

Unity that defies denominations

Another extraordinary hallmark of the movement is its ability to unite Christians from different traditions. In the prayer room, denominational labels fade. Charismatics pray with liturgical believers, evangelicals alongside contemplatives, Pentecostals alongside mainline Protestants, Baptists alongside Anglicans.

The room becomes a space where the body of Christ recognises its shared identity. This unity is not forced; it is natural. When believers focus on Jesus and seek His presence, secondary differences shrink.

The prayer room becomes a picture of heaven, echoing Jesus' prayer in John 17:21, that *"all of them may be one."* Many leaders have commented that the 24-7 prayer movement has fuelled reconciliation between churches in their cities. The pastors are praying together, congregations are now collaborating, mission projects are being shared.

In deeply divided societies - especially across parts of Europe, Africa, and the Middle East - prayer rooms have now become sanctuaries where believers of different backgrounds can meet, forgive each other, and intercede for peace. In a number of cities, weekly prayer gatherings have replaced competitiveness with unity. Churches in the same community that once competed for members now collaborate for the gospel.

The rise of prayer rooms in universities and among the youth

Universities have been one of the most fertile grounds for the movement. At a time when secularism has swept across Western campuses and hostility toward Christianity often runs high, the emergence of prayer rooms has sparked surprising renewal. Students who would never attend a traditional church service have encountered the presence of God when stepping into a quiet prayer room between classes.

Across the UK, Europe, North America, Australia, and parts of Asia, campus 24-7 prayer rooms have resulted in dozens of conversions, spontaneous worship nights, and student-led evangelism. Some universities have reported continuous prayer running for weeks or even months. Professors have been prayed for by name. Dormitories have become mission fields. Bible studies have multiplied. And in several instances, university chaplaincies have been revitalised as students embrace prayer with fresh passion. Teenagers have also been uniquely touched.

Youth ministries around the world report that prayer rooms have become catalysts for deeper discipleship. Instead of teaching prayer as a concept, leaders invite teenagers to pray - to linger, to listen, to worship, to repent, to intercede. The result is often astonishing: spiritual hunger replaces apathy, purity replaces compromise, boldness replaces fear. The movement has restored confidence that the next generation is not lost; it is awakening.

Prayer rooms in difficult places

Perhaps the most moving stories come from prayer rooms established in difficult or dangerous contexts. In the Middle East, small groups of believers - both expatriate workers and local converts - have maintained secret prayer rooms where worship is whispered and written prayers are burned or taken away to avoid discovery. In parts of Africa affected by conflict, prayer rooms have become sanctuaries for traumatised communities - places where people cry out to God for healing and justice.

In Asia, prayer rooms have operated quietly under restrictive regimes, with believers praying through the night for their nation, their government, and persecuted brothers and sisters. These rooms often experience a depth of intercession unmatched in freer environments. The Spirit moves with unusual tenderness and conviction in places where prayer costs more. This global spread reminds the church that prayer is not a luxury; it is essential. It is the lifeblood of spiritual renewal, the engine of mission, and the anchor of hope.

The transformation of ordinary believers

The greatest fruit of the 24-7 Prayer movement is not found in statistics but in transformed lives. Ordinary believers - many of whom had previously struggled with prayer - have discovered intimacy with God. They have learned to hear His voice, to sit in His presence, to intercede for others, to worship freely, and to allow Scripture to shape their desires and decisions. Many testify that prayer rooms became the turning point in their spiritual journey – the catalyst for transformation in their walk with God.

Addictions were broken. Marriages were restored. Callings were clarified. Fears were surrendered. Joy returned. Faith deepened. In prayer, people found what their souls had been seeking. The movement has helped countless believers discover this truth: prayer is not a duty but a relationship. It is not a task but a treasure. It is not a burden but a gift. And it is through the furnace of prayer that God is preparing His church for renewal and mission in the twenty-first century.

A new global prayer culture: Intercession as lifestyle

One of the most striking legacies of the 24-7 Prayer Movement is how it has reshaped the prayer culture of the global church. Before the movement began, many Christians understood prayer primarily in terms of *meetings* - scheduled hour-long gatherings or Wednesday-night intercession groups. But the vision birthed in that first room in Chichester disrupted that paradigm entirely. The 24-7 Movement reframed prayer not as an event but as a *rhythm*, a *presence*, a *habitation*, a *culture*.

This shift is profound. It echoes Paul's clear exhortation: *"Pray continually."* (1 Thessalonians 5:17). For centuries, Christians have struggled with what it means to live this out. The 24-7 Movement offered a practical, lived expression - prayer is not confined to a liturgical slot but woven into the very fabric of the church.

As prayer rooms multiplied worldwide, the effects became clear. churches that once prayed only during crises began cultivating constant intercession. Young people who had never prayed more than a few minutes found themselves lingering for hours in God's presence. Families began prayer rhythms in their homes. Mission teams wove prayer into their daily life, not just before and after ministry.

University students prayed between classes, before exams, and in communal gatherings that went very late into the night. Monasteries and convents, charismatic churches, Pentecostal communities Anglican congregations, and all found common ground in sustained prayer.

This new global prayer culture literally changed everything: the language of worship, the boldness of evangelism, the expectation for revival, and the unity among diverse traditions. It dismantled the idea that prayer must be either contemplative or charismatic - revealing a beautiful blend of both.

In prayer-rooms across many continents, silence and shouting coexisted. Liturgical prayers and also spontaneous intercession complemented each other. Scripture meditation and prophetic worship blended seamlessly. The old categories fell away as the Spirit brought unity through a shared longing for God.

Prayer as fuel for mission movements

Another significant contribution of the 24-7 Movement is the way it energised and sustained mission. While some prayer movements in history leaned toward contemplation or cloistered rhythms, 24-7 Prayer has also combined intercession with radical activism. They speak often of a "monastery and mission" DNA - the belief that intimacy with God fuels transformation in the world, and that prayer without mission is incomplete, just as mission without prayer becomes human effort. This dual emphasis birthed some of the most dynamic mission initiatives of the twenty-first century.

From its earliest years, 24-7 Prayer teams planted missional communities among the marginalised — homeless communities, inner-city neighbourhoods, red-light districts, refugee corridors, and university campuses. They called these "Boiler Rooms," inspired by the Spurgeonian idea that prayer is the furnace powering gospel proclamation. These communities combined daily prayer rhythms with practical service and evangelism. Over time, many evolved into established churches or social-impact ministries.

What began in Europe soon spread to North America, Africa, Asia, and Latin America. The movement became a catalyst for creative mission: artistic outreach, anti-trafficking initiatives, prison ministry, refugee support, and campus revival. All of it saturated in prayer.

This fusion reflects the New Testament model, where prayer and mission are inseparable. In Acts 13:2, the church in Antioch was fasting and worshipping when the Spirit spoke, *"Set apart for me Barnabas and Saul for the work to which I have called them."* Prayer preceded mission, and mission returned continually to prayer. This is precisely the rhythm the 24-7 Movement restored.

The rise of youth-driven revival

As mentioned earlier, one of the most surprising developments of the 24-7 Prayer Movement has been its disproportionately strong impact on young people. Throughout church history, many revivals have been youth-driven, and the 24-7 Movement is no exception. Teenagers and university students flocked to prayer rooms, sensing that they had permission to seek God with raw honesty. They did not need polished liturgy, elaborate programmes, or professional environments. They needed only a room with God.

This openness attracted a whole generation often described as spiritually hungry but institutionally disillusioned. Many young adults had grown up in church but longed for authenticity - something so much deeper than performance-driven services or consumer-oriented Christianity. In 24-7 Prayer rooms, they found a space where God was encountered, not discussed; where the presence of Jesus was tangible; where tears flowed freely; where worship broke out spontaneously; and where Scripture came alive as the Spirit illuminated hearts.

The effects spread across campuses worldwide. Students prayed for friends, professors, entire universities. Evangelism increased, not through programmes but through overflow - students whose hearts had been set ablaze and who could not help but share Christ. Countless testimonies have emerged of dorm-room conversions, late-night prayer walks, and academic buildings becoming places of spiritual breakthrough. This youth-driven dimension positioned the 24-7 Movement as a bridge between generations. Young believers learned to pray from older saints; older believers were strengthened by the passion of youth. It created a multigenerational revival not seen in decades.

Prayer rooms as centres of healing and encounter

As prayer rooms spread globally, one recurring theme appeared: they became places of healing. In many rooms, testimonies emerged of physical healing, emotional restoration, deliverance from anxiety, reconciliation in families, and deep encounters with God's love. The environment of 24-7 rooms - unhurried, scripture-saturated, worship-filled - created space for the Spirit to move in powerful ways.

Some of the most remarkable transformations came from people who had just wandered into prayer rooms unexpectedly. Stories circulated of atheists entering out of curiosity and leaving in tears, of addicts finding freedom, of traumatised refugees experiencing peace, of Pastors burnt-out from ministry encountering renewal, and of people sensing God's presence for the first time.

This phenomenon recalls the promise God made through Jeremiah: *"You will seek me and find me when you seek me with all your heart."* (Jeremiah 29:13). The simplicity of these rooms made that promise accessible. They became modern altars - sacred spaces where the veil felt thin and God's presence unmistakable.

Global unity through the language of prayer

Perhaps one of the most precious outcomes of the 24-7 Prayer Movement is how it brought unprecedented unity among diverse Christian traditions. Pentecostals, Anglicans, Baptists, Catholics, charismatics, Orthodox, and non-denominational communities all found common ground in prayer rooms. Barriers that had existed for centuries seemed less significant in the presence of God.

Prayer became the universal language of unity. It allowed churches that would never collaborate structurally to collaborate spiritually. It joined nations, cultures, and denominations in a shared hunger for revival. Conferences, gatherings, and online prayer chains soon developed, linking tens of thousands of believers across continents.

When crisis struck - a war, a natural disaster, a pandemic - prayer rooms mobilised global intercession within hours. This unity echoes Jesus' longing *"that they may all be one... so that the world may believe."* (John 17:21). In a world fragmented by politics, culture, and ideology, the church found a unifying centre in the presence of God.

A furnace still burning

More than twenty-five years after its unexpected beginning, the 24-7 Prayer Movement continues to burn. It has become a global ecosystem of prayer, mission, creativity, and renewal. Its global influence is seen in church-planting movements, a new worship culture, fresh evangelism strategies, youth revival, digital prayer platforms, and intercession networks that respond to world events in real time.

Yet at its heart, the movement remains surprisingly simple: ordinary people, in ordinary rooms, seeking an extraordinary God - day and night, without ceasing.

And the furnace continues to grow.

8. THE ALPHA COURSE RENEWAL: MILLIONS ENCOUNTERING CHRIST

The story of the Alpha Course is one of the most extraordinary renewal movements of the past thirty years. What began as a modest introductory Christian course in a local London church has become a discipleship and evangelistic phenomenon – crossing cultures, denominations, languages, and generations. More than just a program, Alpha has now become a spiritual ecosystem through which millions have encountered Christ, many for the first time, and countless others have rediscovered the depth of a living relationship with Him.

This chapter explores how God has used Alpha to awaken faith across continents, revitalize churches, unify believers around the gospel, and create spaces where seekers of every background can ask honest questions and experience the presence of the Holy Spirit. It is a movement that blends hospitality, relationship, conversation, prayer, testimony, and the power of the Spirit into a simple but life-changing journey.

A movement born from humble beginnings

The Alpha story begins not in a stadium crusade or a major conference but in the quiet ministry of Holy Trinity Brompton (HTB) in London. In the late twentieth century, HTB sought a fresh way to introduce newcomers to Christianity in a relaxed, relational format. The early version of Alpha focused on essential Christian truths - who Jesus is, why He died, how faith works - but it remained relatively small and contained within church walls. Then God breathed on it.

The turning point came when a renewed emphasis on the Holy Spirit - particularly a dedicated session on the work of the Spirit - was added to the course. What had been primarily instructional suddenly became transformational. Guests did not simply learn about Jesus; many encountered Him. Hearts softened. Tears flowed. Bondages broke. Lives turned. And word spread – not just in London and the UK, but right across the world!

Alpha transitioned from a teaching tool to a kingdom catalyst. churches began to adopt it—first across London, then the UK, then Europe, then the world. The focus was simple: create a safe environment where people can explore faith, experience community, and meet Jesus in a personal way.

Why Alpha works: A culture of welcome

One of the most distinctive features of Alpha - and one of the deepest reasons for its massive global impact - is its emphasis on hospitality. From the moment guests arrive, they are welcomed into an atmosphere of acceptance, warmth, food, friendship, and conversation. Alpha leaders often say, *"People come for the meal, and stay for the message."* Hospitality, for Alpha, is not just an accessory - it is part of the theology. It reflects the heart of Jesus who welcomed strangers, shared meals with outcasts, and invited the weary to come and rest.

This approach resonates across the globe. In bustling cities, remote villages, university campuses, prisons, and corporate boardrooms, the dinner-table model works because it speaks to a universal human need: to belong. Many guests arrive with questions, doubts, fears, or painful experiences with religion. The first step toward transformation is not a lecture, but a welcome.

Jesus said, *"By this everyone will know that you are my disciples, if you love one another."* (John 13:35). Alpha creates that environment of love first - before any teaching begins. And around that relational foundation, the Holy Spirit often moves with surprising power.

A safe place for big questions

Alpha's global success is also grounded in its openness to honest questions. In many different religious environments - Christian or otherwise - questions are discouraged, doubts are shamed, and seekers feel pressured to believe before they understand. Alpha reverses that dynamic. Each session includes a talk and then open discussion in small groups.

No question is off limits. No view is dismissed. No one is forced to agree. The table becomes a space for conversation rather than confrontation. Leaders listen more than they speak. Participants are encouraged to wrestle, explore, debate, and reflect.

This approach has proven uniquely effective in our current age of scepticism and digital information. People are no longer persuaded by authority alone - they are persuaded much more by authenticity. Alpha's honesty meets the cultural moment. It creates space for the Spirit to draw seekers gently rather than forcefully.

Behind this lies Jesus' invitation: *"Come and see"* (John 1:39). Alpha embodies that invitation. It invites guests not to blind belief but to open exploration - trusting that encountering Jesus will ultimately answer their questions more fully than arguments ever could.

The weekend away: A turning point of transformation

Perhaps the most significant feature of Alpha - the moment so many describe as life-changing - is the "Holy Spirit weekend" or "Holy Spirit day." This dedicated session focuses on who the Spirit is, how He works in the life of a believer, and how He empowers Christians for living.

Around the world, testimonies abound of the Spirit moving tenderly and powerfully during this time. People report experiencing God's love deeply for the first time. Some weep as years of pain are released. Others find healing from emotional wounds. Many experience freedom from addictions, anxiety, or spiritual oppression. Countless guests simply describe a profound peace they had never known.

This emphasis on the Spirit aligns with the promise of Jesus we see in Acts 1:8, *"You will receive power when the Holy Spirit comes on you."* Alpha has now become one of the most widespread platforms through which modern Christians - especially those without charismatic church backgrounds - encounter the Spirit in life-transforming ways.

Crossing denominations, cultures, and languages

Another extraordinary element of the Alpha renewal is its cross-denominational nature. Alpha is used by Anglicans, Baptists, Pentecostals, Roman Catholics, independents, Presbyterians, Methodists, and countless other traditions. In many cities now, churches across denominations host Alpha together - finding unity around the essentials of the gospel rather than dividing over secondary differences.

In a fractured Christian world, Alpha becomes a table of reconciliation. It reflects Jesus' prayer: *"that they may be one."* (John 17:11). The shared mission of introducing people to Christ draws believers together and strengthens the witness of the church.

Alpha has also crossed cultures remarkably well. Its format — food, friendship, video content, conversation — translates into almost any context. It has been run in over a hundred languages, in every major global region. The core human needs for connection, meaning, forgiveness, and hope transcend cultural boundaries.

From high-rise apartments in Singapore to villages in India, from prisons in the United States to café gatherings in Europe, from slums in Africa to youth groups in South America, Alpha flourishes because it speaks to the human heart universally.

Stories of encounter and life change

The testimonies emerging from Alpha are countless and diverse:

- A hardened atheist weeps as he experiences God's love for the first time.
- A young woman traumatised by her past finds healing and forgiveness.
- A former gang member discovers purpose and peace.
- A couple on the brink of divorce find restoration through encountering Christ.

- A lonely university student meets Christian peers and discovers belonging.
- A prison inmate experiences the Holy Spirit and becomes a leader in the prison fellowship.
- A businessman realises life's emptiness and surrenders to Jesus.

These stories echo across so many nations. Alpha is not merely transferring information - it is facilitating a transformation. It creates room for the gospel to be heard, for the Spirit to be experienced, and for lives to be changed. The global church is witnessing through Alpha what the early disciples witnessed in Acts: when Christ is proclaimed simply, authentically, and relationally, hearts open and the Spirit moves.

A global framework that transcends culture

One of the most remarkable aspects of the Alpha Course is its cross-cultural adaptability. Unlike many evangelistic tools that require significant contextual modification, Alpha seems almost uniquely flexible. It flourishes in Western secular cities, African townships, East Asian metropolises, Pacific Islands, Middle Eastern diaspora groups, rural villages, university campuses, prisons, corporate offices, and military bases. Its ability to inhabit diverse environments without losing theological clarity has made it one of the most influential evangelistic tools in modern history.

Part of this adaptability lies in Alpha's relational posture. The course assumes that people everywhere have deep questions about life, purpose, meaning, suffering, hope, and identity. Alpha does not begin with doctrinal assertions, but with a hospitable invitation: *"You are welcome here. Bring your questions. Let's explore this together."* For many seekers - especially those disillusioned by institutional religion - this tone is refreshing.

Alpha's structure also translates universally. A shared meal, a thought-provoking talk, and open small-group discussion reflect basic human rhythms.

Nearly every culture values conversation, community, and hospitality. These elements disarm defensiveness and create a safe space for spiritual exploration. As the apostle Paul wrote, *"I have become all things to all people so that by all possible means I might save some."* (1 Corinthians 9:22). Alpha captures the spirit of this verse by removing unnecessary barriers and making the gospel accessible.

Another factor is Alpha's use of storytelling. Rather than relying on abstract theology, Alpha weaves personal testimonies, real-world examples, and honest reflection throughout its sessions. This resonates deeply across cultures. Stories have universal power. They carry truth in ways that reach the heart before the intellect, inviting listeners into a larger narrative - God's story of redemption.

Above all, Alpha resonates because it places Jesus at the centre. Whether in Nairobi, Buenos Aires, London, Delhi, or Seoul, the heart of the course is the person of Christ: who He is, why He came, why He died, and what it means to follow Him. Amid global diversity, this message remains constant. As Jesus Himself said, *"And I, when I am lifted up from the earth, will draw all people to myself."* (John 12:32). Alpha lifts up Jesus - and He draws the people in.

The Holy Spirit weekend: The turning point

As mentioned above, if Alpha is known for anything beyond its hospitality and discussion, it is known for the "Holy Spirit weekend" — often described as the heart of the course, the point where information becomes encounter. This retreat typically occurs around week seven and focuses on three sessions: *Who is the Holy Spirit? What does the Holy Spirit do? How can I be filled with the Holy Spirit?*

Across denominations, cultures, and continents, this weekend has been the catalyst for countless transformative experiences. Many who began Alpha as sceptics or agnostics describe this retreat as the moment everything shifted — when faith moved from theory to reality.

In London, participants speak of moments of overwhelming peace, tears of joy, or an unexpected sense of God's presence. In Brazil, worship during the retreat often erupts into passionate singing, heartfelt prayer, and visible expressions of repentance and renewal. In East Africa, attendees describe reconciliation, healing, and restored relationships. In East Asia, testimonies frequently involve quiet yet undeniable encounters with the love of God - a deep inner assurance that Jesus is real and present.

These experiences are not without theological grounding. Alpha teaches that the Holy Spirit is the Comforter and Advocate whom Jesus promised to send to us (John 14:16–17). It points participants to the biblical pattern of believers being filled with the Spirit for guidance, transformation, and mission. And significantly, Alpha emphasises that the Spirit's work is rooted in Scripture, not emotionalism. Participants are invited to encounter the Spirit personally, but always through prayer, teaching, and discernment.

This emphasis has revitalised many churches. For congregations that had drifted into dryness or routine, the Holy Spirit weekend often becomes a spark of renewal. Many pastors report that as their people experience God afresh, worship deepens, prayer intensifies, and mission becomes joyful rather than dutiful. In this way, Alpha serves as both an evangelistic tool and a renewal movement within the church itself.

Alpha in secular cities: A quiet revolution

One of the greatest surprises of the Alpha movement has been its effectiveness in highly secularised, post-Christian environments. In cities like London, Vancouver, Melbourne, Amsterdam, and Copenhagen - places where traditional evangelism often falls flat - Alpha has thrived. It offers a non-threatening, relational entry point for those who are spiritually curious but institutionally wary. In many secular contexts, people feel safe attending Alpha because it is not a church service. It does not demand immediate commitment. It welcomes scepticism and questions. In a culture shaped by individualism and post-modern suspicion of authority, Alpha meets people where they are.

A striking example is the explosion of Alpha in central London in the 1990s and early 2000s, particularly HTB. As thousands of young professionals found faith through Alpha, a spiritual renewal began that influenced churches across the UK. Out of this, HTB's church-planting network emerged - a movement that revitalised ageing parishes, reinvigorated worship, and brought new life to neighbourhoods previously disconnected from Christianity.

The pattern has been repeated right across the globe. In Canada, hundreds of churches adopted Alpha as their primary outreach tool, leading to testimonies of atheists coming to faith, marriages restored, addictions broken, and communities transformed. In Australia and New Zealand, Alpha has attracted university students, young professionals, and even business leaders, many of whom were previously indifferent or hostile to Christianity.

The genius of Alpha in secular contexts is that it removes pressure. People come not to be preached at, but to explore. They are not asked to agree, but to consider. They are not pushed to believe but invited to encounter. And in that safe, hospitable environment, the gospel speaks with surprising clarity.

Alpha in the majority world: Multiplying disciples

While Alpha has made a profound impact in the West, some of its most significant growth has occurred in the Global South. In nations across Africa, Asia, and Latin America, the course has become a powerful catalyst for discipleship and community transformation.

In Africa, Alpha's communal approach fits naturally within cultures that value hospitality, story, and shared learning. churches across Ghana, Zambia, Nigeria, and Kenya use Alpha to disciple new believers, strengthen families, and unify congregations.

The Holy Spirit weekend often becomes a moment of cultural and spiritual breakthrough - blending local expressions of worship with the global body of Christ.

In India, Alpha is used across denominations and languages. Its emphasis on conversation resonates in a culture where dialogue is a deeply embedded social value. Many Indian churches use Alpha not only for evangelism but for leadership development, small-group formation, and healing ministry.

In Southeast Asia, Alpha has been pivotal in building bridges across cultures and generations. Urban professionals, rural families, expatriates, and migrant workers have all found Alpha to be a meaningful space for exploring faith.

The key insight here is this: Alpha succeeds because it does not impose a foreign style of Christianity. It offers a simple, relational framework - and communities adapt it to their own rhythms, languages, and traditions. Thus, Alpha becomes not a Western export, but a global tool shaped by local believers.

Alpha in prisons: Hope behind bars

One of the most extraordinary manifestations of the Alpha Renewal has occurred inside prisons. Alpha began being used in UK prisons decades ago and has since spread to correctional facilities around the world. The impact has been astonishing.

Prisoners often arrive at Alpha hardened, distrustful, or hopeless. But in the environment of honest conversation and non-judgmental welcome, they soften. Many describe encountering forgiveness for the first time. Others speak of chains breaking - spiritual, emotional, or behavioural.

Inmates frequently complete the course and then begin leading Alpha groups for newcomers. Some continue the journey after release, becoming leaders in churches, communities, or recovery ministries.

Alpha in prisons demonstrates one of the most powerful truths of the gospel: no one is beyond the reach of Christ's love. Jesus' words ring true: *"If the Son sets you free, you will be free indeed."* (John 8:36).

The power of conversation in a distracted age

In a world marked by division, overstimulation, and the constant noise of digital life, Alpha taps into a deep need: the desire to be heard. Modern life has created an epidemic of loneliness. People scroll endlessly through social feeds yet feel disconnected. They are surrounded by opinions yet starved of meaningful dialogue. They hear slogans but rarely experience conversation that touches the heart. Alpha offers the opposite. It provides a safe, structured environment where people can speak openly without fear of judgment. Participants are invited to share their doubts, fears, hopes, and questions. There is no pressure to agree. No expectation to pretend. The tone is gentle, the pace unhurried. And because of this environment, people begin saying things they have carried inside for years.

A pastor in Germany once said, *"Alpha is the only place in our church where non-Christians talk more than Christians."* This is by design. Alpha understands that spiritual transformation often begins with honest questions. Jesus Himself frequently asked questions that unlocked deep conversations:

"Who do you say I am?" (Matthew 16:15)
"What do you want me to do for you?" (Mark 10:51)
"Do you want to get well?" (John 5:6)

These questions were not rhetorical - they were invitations to encounter truth personally. Alpha's environment of open dialogue allows participants to wrestle with faith in community. Many people today are not rejecting Christianity - they are rejecting a caricature of it. They have never actually had a safe space to explore who Jesus is. Alpha provides that space. And in doing so, it has become a lifeline for a generation searching for something real.

Hospitality as evangelism

Hospitality lies at the heart of Alpha's impact. Every session begins with a shared meal - not as an icebreaker, but as ministry. Food creates community. It lowers defences.

It invites people to relax. It builds trust. Scripture presents hospitality as a powerful expression of God's love. *"Practice hospitality."* (Romans 12:13). *"Do not forget to show hospitality to strangers."* (Hebrews 13:2). Alpha takes these exhortations very seriously.

In countless settings, from small town halls to bustling inner-city churches, volunteers gather hours before the session begins to prepare meals. Their service is an act of love - silent yet powerful. Many participants later say that the meal was the moment they began to trust the process. It communicated something words never could: *"You matter. You are welcome here."*

In cultures where hospitality is deeply ingrained - such as the Middle East, Latin America, and parts of Africa - Alpha resonates even more strongly. The shared meal becomes a bridge for the gospel. In cultures that have lost communal rhythms - such as parts of Western Europe and North America - Alpha reintroduces them, reminding people of the joy and warmth of sitting at a table together.

Alpha's surprising appeal to the secular and the sceptical

One of Alpha's most fascinating developments is its resonance among people who describe themselves as *"spiritual but not religious,"* agnostic, or even atheist. In some of the most secular nations in the world - Sweden, the Netherlands, New Zealand, and parts of the UK - Alpha thrives. Why?

Because Alpha lowers barriers. It offers safety before it offers answers. It creates belonging before belief. It recognises the emotional, intellectual, and relational complexity of modern life. It respects people's stories rather than rushing them toward conclusions. In many ways, Alpha has become a cultural interpreter - helping secular people see that Christianity is not an institution to escape but a relationship to discover.

Alpha also appeals to intelligent seekers. Its content is coherent, historically grounded, and intellectually rigorous without being academic.

It introduces people to the evidence for Christianity, the reliability of Scripture, the identity of Jesus, and the logic of the gospel. Many participants remark that they had never heard Christianity explained so clearly. For secular professionals - doctors, lawyers, teachers, business leaders - Alpha offers an accessible pathway into faith. For university students, it provides a safe space to ask difficult questions. For sceptics, it offers a respectful environment where doubt is welcomed rather than criticised. In a world suspicious of religious pressure, Alpha is refreshingly non-coercive.

A course with global scalability

One of the reasons Alpha has reached millions is its scalability. It does not require expensive technology, specialised venues, or professional speakers. A small rural church can run Alpha as effectively as a large cathedral. A prison can host Alpha just as fruitfully as a university campus. A living room can become an Alpha venue. So can a refugee camp. The model is simple but profound - easily reproducible and adaptable. This scalability has enabled Alpha to spread into surprising environments:

- Prisons across multiple nations
- Military bases
- Rehabilitation centres
- Homeless shelters
- Corporate offices
- High schools and universities
- Digital platforms for online groups
- House-church networks in restricted nations

In each context, the course remains the same, but the expression adapts to the needs of the community. And the fruit remains undeniable. The next section will explore Alpha's influence within churches, the renewal it has brought to congregations, and the way it has bridged many denominational divides in an unprecedented way.

A family shaped by hospitality, humility, and the Holy Spirit

As the Alpha Course matured, its deepest strength began to emerge - not simply as an evangelistic programme but as a culture of hospitality, listening, vulnerability, and dependence on the Holy Spirit. This culture became the beating heart of Alpha's whole effectiveness, drawing people across cultures, denominations, and backgrounds to explore the Christian faith in a space that felt unexpectedly safe and radically open.

At the centre of this culture is a simple principle: the table matters. Alpha meals, whether lavish or simple, whether home-cooked or store-bought, create an atmosphere in which strangers become friends, sceptics feel heard, and barriers begin to break down.

Across continents, Alpha teams discovered that a shared meal places everyone on equal footing - pastors, seekers, atheists, agnostics, Muslims, former Christians, and the spiritually curious. The conversation becomes human, relational, honest.

This emphasis on hospitality echoes the ministry of Jesus, who so often taught and revealed Himself at tables - breaking bread with tax collectors, Pharisees, sinners, the overlooked and the unworthy.

It reflects the early church's rhythm of gathering *"from house to house"* and sharing meals *"with glad and sincere hearts"* (Acts 2:46). The table becomes an altar of grace, a place where God moves quietly yet powerfully.

But hospitality alone would never have sustained Alpha's global momentum. The second defining mark is humility - a posture of openness, listening, and genuine curiosity. Alpha leaders quickly realised that heavy-handed persuasion repelled people.

What drew seekers in was the invitation to express doubts, ask questions, and be honest about their struggles. Alpha's strength is not its ability to answer every question, but its confidence that Jesus Himself will meet people in the journey.

This humility is woven into every aspect of the course. Leaders do not attempt to dominate discussions or correct every misunderstanding. Instead, they create space—trusting that the Holy Spirit works best in environments where people feel safe to explore faith without fear of judgment. In a world increasingly marked by polarisation, suspicion, and defensiveness, such an environment feels startlingly refreshing.

The third defining dimension is the most transformative: that is our dependence on the Holy Spirit. While Alpha is structured, hospitable, and well organised, the power of the movement has always rested on God Himself. Which is why the Holy Spirit weekend became the signature turning point in countless lives.

This Holy Spirit-dependent dimension explains why Alpha transcended denominational boundaries. The course did not ask churches to change their theology or liturgy—it simply created a pathway for people to encounter Jesus personally and experience the work of the Spirit. In that sense, Alpha became a unifying force in a fragmented Christian landscape.

A movement that continues to evolve

Another key to Alpha's longevity is its willingness to adapt without losing its core. As cultures shift, Alpha has expanded into new formats - Alpha Youth, Alpha in Prisons, Alpha Chinese, corporate Alpha, Alpha Marriage, Alpha Digital, and more. These adaptations have allowed the course to remain relevant while staying faithful to its foundational vision: helping people encounter Jesus.

This flexibility became especially evident during seasons of global crisis - like the global Covid pandemic. When lockdowns shuttered churches and gatherings across continents, many assumed Alpha would be forced to pause. Instead, the movement rapidly transitioned online. Within weeks, churches around the world were hosting these digital Alpha courses, discovering that seekers who would never walk into a church building were willing to join a Zoom call from their living room.

Online Alpha removed barriers of geography, transportation, social anxiety, and family dynamics. People from different countries joined the same course. Parents with young children participated easily. Those with disabilities or health concerns found new accessibility. And in countless stories, the Holy Spirit moved powerfully - even through a screen. Many church leaders described online Alpha as *"the most fruitful season we have ever seen."*

This adaptability reflects the Spirit-filled wisdom of the early church. When persecution scattered the believers, the gospel spread (Acts 8:4). When obstacles arose, the Spirit opened new doors. Alpha's evolution mirrors this pattern: creativity grounded in dependence on God.

Why Alpha matters for the twenty-first century church

In a world marked by disconnection, suspicion, and cultural polarisation, Alpha offers something deeply countercultural: **a** safe table, a listening ear, an open heart, and a clear invitation to know Jesus. These elements make Alpha uniquely suited to the spiritual landscape of our era.

People today do not merely want information - they want relationship. They do not simply want arguments - they search for authenticity. They do not only want answers - they want real encounters with the living God. Alpha brings these elements together in a way that bridges divides and draws the spiritually curious toward Christ. It embodies a truth many churches are rediscovering: evangelism is not a programme but a culture. Renewal is not manufactured but welcomed. Conversion is not coerced but birthed by the Spirit. And hospitality - the simple act of sitting at a table with strangers who may one day become family - can change the world.

Alpha's story continues to unfold across nations, languages, and denominations. It is a living testimony that God still meets people today in ways that are not only personal, but powerful, and transformative.

9. DIGITAL DISCIPLESHIP: HOW ONLINE MINISTRY IS TRANSFORMING GLOBAL FAITH

Long before the concept became mainstream, many believers quietly sensed that the internet would one day become one of the greatest tools for evangelism and discipleship the world had ever known. Today, that intuition has become an exciting reality. Across continents, cultures, languages and generations, the gospel is spreading 24 hours a day through online platforms at an unprecedented pace. What began as just small experiments - churches posting sermons online, Christian forums hosting Q&A sessions, email-based devotionals - has now grown into a global digital movement touching millions of people every day.

This chapter explores how God is moving through this online ministry: transforming evangelism, deepening discipleship, expanding prayer movements, and creating new forms of Christian community that transcend borders. It is a story of innovation, resilience, opportunity and grace - a story of the gospel entering the digital highways and finding hungry hearts waiting.

From websites to waves of revival

The digital revolution began quietly. In the early years of the internet, Christians began posting testimonies, Bible teachings and worship songs online. But nobody could have foreseen the scale of transformation that would follow. As technology advanced, bandwidth increased, and smartphones spread across the world, the reach of digital ministry exploded.

Today, billions of people carry smartphones - devices capable of streaming sermons, Bible apps, prayer rooms, discipleship courses, evangelistic videos and full online worship services. Regions which were once difficult to reach with our traditional missionary methods are now accessible through mobile screens. Doors previously closed by political restrictions or cultural barriers are quietly opening through digital channels.

What makes this moment remarkable is that online ministry is not merely an add-on to physical church life. It has become a primary avenue through which countless seekers encounter Christ. Many first hear the gospel not through a preacher in a pulpit but through a video clip, a social media post, a livestreamed service, or a conversation with a Christian mentor online. In God's providence, the digital world has become a modern *"marketplace of Athens"* - a worldwide space where ideas are exchanged, hearts are open, and truth travels quickly.

Evangelism in the digital age

Online evangelism has become one of the most fruitful mission fields in the world. This is not because the internet is inherently spiritual, but because it is inherently human. Behind every screen is a person longing for connection, identity, hope and truth. The global church has witnessed several significant developments:

1. *Search-based evangelism*
   Millions of people search questions like *"Who is Jesus?"*, *"Does God love me?"*, or *"How can I overcome anxiety?"* Online ministries respond to these questions with Bible-based truths, testimonies and invitations to know Christ.

2. *Social media testimony*
   Ordinary believers share faith stories, Scripture verses and reflections on platforms like YouTube, Instagram, TikTok and Facebook. Many report that seekers message them privately - often from closed countries - asking about Jesus.

3. *Evangelistic video content*
   Short clips of worship, teaching or testimony reach audiences who would never attend a church service. For some, a 60-second video becomes the moment God uses to soften a hardened heart.

4. *Digital missionaries*
   Christians trained in online evangelism engage seekers in one-on-one conversations, answering questions, praying and guiding them toward faith.

In all of this, the Spirit is at work. The gospel is crossing borders without passports, entering nations where missionaries cannot travel, and reaching individuals who would never step into a church building.

Bible access without barriers

The digital age has given the world something previous generations could scarcely imagine: instant access to Scripture. Bible apps, downloadable audio Bibles, video devotionals and Bible reading plans now reach millions daily. In countries where printed Bibles are banned or restricted, believers download the Bible to their phones, sometimes at great risk. In underground networks, digital Scripture has become a lifeline - small, discreet, and difficult for authorities to control.

Searchable, shareable and translated into hundreds of languages, the Bible is more accessible today than at any point in human history. The promise of God is being fulfilled in real time: *"the word of God is not chained."* (2 Timothy 2:9).

Online discipleship that changes lives

While evangelism often begins online, discipleship increasingly continues there. Digital platforms now host:

- one-on-one mentoring
- virtual small groups
- interactive Bible studies
- theology courses
- prayer partnerships
- support networks for new believers
- pastoral counselling

This is especially transformative in regions where public Christian gatherings are dangerous or impossible. Believers can be discipled without leaving their homes. They can grow in Scripture, receive encouragement, ask questions and share struggles - all without physical exposure.

The digital environment also enables Christians from different nations to disciple one another. A pastor in Kenya may mentor new believers in Europe. A missionary in Brazil may lead an online Bible study with seekers in Asia. The global church becomes interconnected in ways never seen before.

Prayer without borders

Digital prayer rooms and livestreamed intercession gatherings have become global phenomena. Believers from dozens of nations join online to pray for revival, missions, healing and spiritual breakthrough. This represents a new expression of Jesus' words: *"My house will be called a house of prayer for all nations."* (Mark 11:17).

Prayer is no longer limited by geography. The *"upper room"* has gone global. Believers pray together in real time, interceding across time zones and continents. Digital prayer chains run 24 hours a day, 7 days a week. Many report powerful experiences of unity, presence and encouragement.

Worship for a connected world

Online worship has also become a significant part of global Christian life. Worship videos, livestreamed services and digital concerts bring worship into homes, hospitals, prisons, dormitories and refugee camps. For millions, these digital gatherings have become their primary place of connection with the church.

What makes online worship remarkable is not performance but accessibility. Anyone, anywhere - using nothing more than a phone - can join the song of heaven. Worship transcends the screen; hearts are lifted, tears are shed, prayers rise, and Christ is exalted.

Community in the digital wilderness

Many people assume that online church cannot provide real community. Yet thousands now testify that digital Christian fellowship has become their spiritual family.

This is especially true for:

- isolated believers
- the disabled
- the persecuted
- shift-workers
- travellers
- those without local churches
- new believers in restricted nations

Digital communities are not virtual substitutes - they are real expressions of the body of Christ, bound not by proximity but by the Spirit.

A global move of God in cyberspace

The digital revolution is not a technological accident. It is a sovereign opportunity. God is using the internet to draw millions to Christ, disciple them deeply, gather them into community, and mobilise them for mission. It is one of the great moves of God in our current time - quiet, vast, borderless and unstoppable.

When renewal moves outside the church walls

One of the defining features of the current global renewal is that a considerable portion of it is happening outside traditional church environments. This is not because the church has become irrelevant, but because the Spirit of God is moving freely into places where people actually live their daily lives — workplaces, homes, community spaces, cafés, prisons, university campuses, parks, and digital environments. The walls that once separated the 'sacred' from the 'secular' are dissolving as believers discover that God meets people wherever they are.

In many Western nations where formal church attendance has declined, spiritual hunger has not disappeared - it has simply moved elsewhere. People are exploring their own faith through conversations, creative expressions, online communities, films, podcasts, and friendships.

Younger generations are now seeking authenticity more than formality, and they respond to spirituality that is relational, experiential, and integrated with life. This shift mirrors the ministry of Jesus. He taught in synagogues, yes, but He also taught on hillsides, in fishing boats, at dinner tables, beside wells, and in marketplaces. The book of Acts continues this pattern - faith spreading in homes, public squares, workshops, and prisons. Renewal today looks much the same. It is relational, decentralised, and woven into the fabric of everyday life.

Think of the apostle Paul's words: *"In him we live and move and have our being."* (Acts 17:28). God's presence does not wait for a building. He is present wherever people are open to encounter Him. In this new wave of global renewal, the everyday spaces of life are becoming altars and classrooms of transformation. Believers around the world are rediscovering a simple but powerful truth: revival is not confined to Sunday gatherings. It is carried by ordinary Christians in daily life.

Transformational conversations: One person at a time

If the twentieth century emphasised mass evangelism - stadiums filled, crusades launched, microphones lifted - the twenty-first century is witnessing the rise of something more intimate: transformational conversations. These are just simple, authentic, Spirit-led conversations where Christians can listen deeply, speak gently, and carry the presence of Christ into relationships.

In cafés and workplaces across the West, conversations about spirituality, meaning, grief, purpose, anxiety, and hope are becoming opportunities for evangelism - not in the traditional sense of a structured presentation, but in the natural flow of friendship. Many people who would never walk into a church are opening up to Jesus because someone took time to listen, care, and speak truth with humility.

Across Europe, for example, churches involved in the "missional communities" movement focus not on attracting crowds, but on forming small groups around shared activities - cycling clubs, book circles, parenting groups, community gardens, or just neighbourhood meals.

Through friendship, trust, and love, conversations emerge that lead people to Christ. It is gentle evangelism, which is rooted in relationship and marked by authenticity.

In the United States, studies show that a significant percentage of young adults exploring faith do so not because of programmes but because of friendships—relationships with believers who displayed integrity, kindness, and spiritual reality. The witness of a life transformed is more compelling than any event.

This mirrors the New Testament pattern, where the gospel spread primarily through households, friendships, and networks of trust. When Andrew met Jesus, the first thing he did was bring his brother Simon (John 1:40–42). Evangelism began with a conversation and a relationship—and that is precisely what is happening again today.

Digital pathways: How the internet has become a mission field

Another major feature of global renewal is the rise of digital evangelism. The internet has become one of the most significant mission fields in human history. People are searching for meaning, answers, hope, and spiritual truth online - and millions of them are encountering Christ in digital spaces.

Podcasts exploring the Christian faith attract millions of listeners. YouTube channels sharing testimonies, Bible teaching, apologetics, and worship have become lifelines for seekers. Many Muslims exploring Christianity begin their journey through digital content long before they ever meet a believer. Across Asia, Africa, the Middle East, and the West, online ministries are seeing unprecedented engagement.

The digital environment also allows seekers to explore faith privately and safely, especially in nations where Christianity is restricted. A person can explore Scripture, prayer, and church life anonymously - until they feel safe to connect personally. Even social media platforms, often seen as shallow or divisive, are being redeemed as spaces where believers share testimonies, Scripture, prayers, and stories of hope.

The Holy Spirit is using reels, videos, livestreams, messages, and online communities to draw people to Christ. Digital pathways are not replacements for real community - but they are often powerful doorways into it.

A countercultural witness

As modern society becomes increasingly frenetic, many Christians - especially younger generations - are craving deeper spiritual rhythms. Out of this deep hunger has emerged the rediscovery of new monasticism: small, intentional Christian communities seeking to live out ancient practices in modern contexts. These communities emphasise prayer, shared meals, simplicity, justice, hospitality, and deep spiritual friendship.

Across the UK, Europe, Australia, and North America, these neo-monastic groups are offering a countercultural alternative to consumer Christianity. They anchor their lives in fixed-hour prayer, Scripture, confession, and acts of mercy. Some operate community houses; others gather weekly for spiritual rhythms while living in separate homes.

This movement is not about withdrawal, but engagement. It reflects the teaching of Jesus: "Let your light shine before others" (Matthew 5:16). By living visibly different lives - marked by peace, generosity, simplicity, and prayer - these communities become living witnesses to the kingdom of God.

Their influence, while subtle, is spreading. Many seekers drawn to contemplative spirituality or social justice initiatives find in these communities an authentic expression of Christ's love.

Everyday missionaries

Perhaps the most encouraging aspect of the global renewal happening outside church structures is this: ordinary Christians are discovering that they are missionaries where they already are. Teachers, nurses, business owners, builders, students, retirees, artists, athletes, parents - all are awakening to the truth that mission is not an activity that is reserved for pastors or professionals. It is the calling of every follower of Jesus.

This is the re-emergence of the priesthood of all believers which Peter wrote about in 1 Peter 2:9. And as it has awakened globally, renewal has spread far beyond church walls. Faith has entered boardrooms, classrooms, cafés, hospitals, gyms, parks, and homes. The joy, peace, and presence of Christ carried by ordinary believers has become a living testimony. This reality is transforming the face of Christianity in much of the Western world. Instead of relying solely on clergy, churches are now equipping every member to pray, serve, witness, and disciple others. The fruit is remarkable: growth rooted in everyday life.

A global shift in how people encounter Christ

Across continents, one theme is becoming clear: the Spirit of God is not waiting for people to come to church. He is moving into the rhythms of daily life. He is now meeting people in quiet conversations, unexpected moments, online searches, spiritual curiosity, and relational networks.

We are living in a time when the mission field and the daily world have become one and the same. The church is rediscovering that mission is not a programme - it is a lifestyle. Renewal is not something we pray for "out there" - it is something God is doing through His people wherever they go.

And this is perhaps the greatest sign of all: global renewal is not limited to extraordinary events or world-famous leaders. It is happening now through ordinary believers, in ordinary places, through ordinary moments, all filled with the extraordinary presence of God.

Depth in a distracted age

As online ministry expands across continents, a crucial question emerges: can genuine discipleship happen digitally? For many years, Christian leaders assumed discipleship required physical proximity - face-to-face meetings, shared meals, small groups in homes, and gathered worship. These are profoundly important. But the digital revolution has demonstrated that discipleship can also flourish in unexpected places: in direct messages, video calls, livestream chats, WhatsApp groups, and online cohorts that span nations and time zones.

In countries where persecution prevents public gatherings, online discipleship is not optional—it is the only safe way to grow in faith. Believers quietly access Scripture through apps, join encrypted pastoral groups, or receive teaching from pastors on the other side of the world. This digital scaffolding allows isolated believers to thrive spiritually even while physically alone.

In the wider world, a generation raised in a digital environment finds it natural to engage spiritually online. They ask questions through Instagram stories. They join prayer groups through Facebook. They participate in Bible studies on Zoom. They find accountability partners through Christian platforms. For them, digital space does not replace real life - it is part of real life.

Though virtual, this discipleship is certainly not shallow. Many pastors (including me!) report that digital seekers ask deeper, more vulnerable questions online than they often do in person. Behind a screen, people feel safe enough to admit doubt, confess sin, express pain, or ask questions they might feel embarrassed to ask in a church foyer. This honesty creates precious rich soil for great spiritual growth.

Digital discipleship embraces a hybrid model: online connection leads to deeper community, which then leads to face-to-face relationships when possible. churches that understand this rhythm find themselves disciple-making seven days a week, not just Sunday mornings. And the fruit is remarkable. One pastor recently commented, *"I have discipled more people through forty-minute video calls than I did in years of traditional programs."* For the first time in history, geography no longer limits the Great Commission.

Online evangelists: A new kind of missionary

The rise of digital ministry has given birth to a new category of gospel worker: the online evangelist. These are men and women who intentionally engage digital spaces with the same missionary heart that church planters carry when they move into a new neighbourhood.

Their "mission field" is not a village or region - it is a digital ecosystem. Some of these evangelists operate on social platforms, creating short, powerful gospel videos that reach millions. Others run Q&A livestreams where seekers can ask real-time questions about faith, Scripture, or suffering. Still others host digital "listening rooms" - spaces where unbelievers share their stories and struggles without fear of judgement.

This digital evangelism has led to countless conversions across nations that remain closed to traditional missions. In some countries, seekers who cannot openly attend a church or own a Bible watch livestreamed baptisms, hear testimonies from around the world, or join online worship gatherings that inspire them to follow Christ secretly.

These online evangelists function like digital versions of the Apostle Paul - travelling into the public squares of the internet, reasoning with people daily about Christ. Their ministry fulfils the spirit of the apostle's words in 1 Corinthians 9:22: *"I have become all things to all people so that by all possible means I might save some."* Today, *"all possible means"* includes online algorithms, livestreams, and secure message links.

The rise of micro-churches and hybrid communities

Another remarkable development within the digital Great Commission is the emergence of hybrid micro-churches - small communities anchored in physical spaces but sustained and expanded through online connection. These groups gather in homes, coffee shops, workplaces, or even rooftops, while maintaining constant online communication throughout the week.

In regions hostile to Christianity, these hybrid micro-churches often function entirely underground. A group of believers may never meet in a large gathering, yet they disciple one another daily through online prayer times, Scripture-reading plans, and video fellowship. This flexibility allows the church to thrive even under severe pressure.

In post-Christian nations, micro-churches reach those who feel unwelcome or uninterested in traditional church settings. They provide intimate, relational spaces for seekers who would never step into a formal service. Digital communication supports these communities by reducing isolation, maintaining momentum, and supporting leaders who often serve bi-vocationally.

In rapidly growing nations, micro-church networks multiply far faster than traditional congregations could. Online training equips new leaders. Shared digital resources provide teaching. Centralised prayer meetings unite dozens or hundreds of micro-communities across cities.

This hybrid model does not diminish the importance of the gathered church. Instead, it extends its reach. It turns every living room into a potential mission base and every smartphone into a discipleship tool. Through these small, flexible gatherings, the church becomes both grounded and global.

Social media as a mission field of unprecedented scale

Social media is vast, noisy, and often spiritually chaotic - but it is also a mission field of unprecedented scale. Every day, billions scroll through content looking for meaning, connection, or escape. Into this restless space, God is raising up believers with the courage to speak the truth, to offer hope, and tell stories of transformation – always pointing people toward Jesus.

Short-form videos have recently become one of the most effective evangelistic tools of the modern age. Testimonies shared in 30-60 seconds can reach people who would never watch a sermon. A single clip explaining a verse or offering a prayer can reach multitudes who would never attend a church service.

Social media bypasses gatekeepers, algorithms become unexpected allies, and gospel seeds scatter across regions no missionary could physically enter. This is not accidental. The Spirit of God is moving through platforms that were never designed for discipleship but are now being redeemed for it.

The challenges of digital ministry

Yet digital ministry is not without challenges. The online world is saturated with misinformation, false teaching, distraction, and spiritual noise. Not every voice that claims to speak for God does so faithfully. Digital discipleship must therefore emphasise discernment, grounding believers in Scripture, community, and wise spiritual authority.

Mental-health struggles, attention fragmentation, online abuse and hostility, and the performance pressures of social media can weigh heavily on digital evangelists. churches must support them with prayer, accountability, and practical care. Healthy boundaries are essential. Spiritual maturity must grow alongside digital reach.

But none of these challenges should outweigh the incredible opportunity before us. The church is learning to wield digital tools responsibly, thoughtfully, and prayerfully. And through this careful stewardship, the gospel continues to advance.

The future of global evangelisation

Looking to the future, online ministry is poised to become one of the most significant evangelistic forces of the twenty-first century. Artificial intelligence, immersive virtual environments, translation technology, and decentralised networks will reshape how the gospel is heard and shared. Language barriers will fall. Remote regions will gain access to resources once reserved for theological libraries. Pastors will shepherd congregations across continents. Discipleship will happen in ways no previous generation could imagine.

Yet the heart of the mission remains unchanged. Jesus' mandate still stands: *"Go and make disciples of all nations"* (Matthew 28:19). What has changed is the way *"all nations"* can now be reached. Through digital platforms, the church can enter homes, hospitals, refugee camps, prisons, and university dorms without visas, permits, or physical travel. A single believer with a phone and a Bible can now reach a thousand people in an afternoon.

This is not a technological triumph - it is a missional revolution. It is the Spirit breathing through cables, screens, satellites, and servers. It is the gospel running along pathways the world never intended for it. It is the church rising in creativity, courage, and compassion for a digital generation longing for truth and belonging.

10. THE TORONTO BLESSING (1994): RIPPLES THROUGH THE 21ST CENTURY

On a cold Thursday evening, on 20 January 1994, in a modest warehouse-style building near Toronto's Pearson International Airport, a small congregation gathered for what they expected would be an ordinary service. The Toronto Airport Vineyard church - pastored by John and Carol Arnott - was not famous, wealthy, or large. It was simply a local church hungry for a fresh touch from God. Their guest speaker that night was Randy Clark, a pastor from St. Louis who himself had only recently undergone a renewal experience in the Holy Spirit. He arrived feeling nervous, even reluctant, yet the leadership sensed God was about to do something unusual.

What unfolded that night - and in the days, weeks, and years that followed - became one of the most significant revival movements of the late twentieth century. The events at Toronto would ignite a global tsunami of renewal that continued shaping churches, networks, ministries, worship styles, missions, and spiritual expectations years after the crowds had dispersed. *The Toronto Blessing,* as it became known, remains a watershed moment in global Christianity.

The night that changed everything

Eyewitnesses recall that as Clark finished preaching and began a simple ministry invitation, the atmosphere in the room shifted. People started weeping. Others laughed with overwhelming joy. Some fell to the floor under what they described as the weight of God's presence. A few trembled or shook. Many simply stood quietly, feeling washed in a deep, fatherly love.

There was no manipulation, no emotive build-up, no dramatic music. Worship was gentle and unstructured. Ministry teams moved softly around the room. Yet the intensity was undeniable. What struck so many was not merely the physical manifestations but the inner transformation occurring in hearts. People testified to huge burdens lifting, wounds healing, fears dissolving, and a profound sense of being loved - truly loved - for the first time.

News spread quickly. The following night the crowd doubled. Within weeks, visitors began flying into Toronto from across Canada, the United States, the United Kingdom, Europe, South Africa, Australia, New Zealand, and South Korea.

Some churches sent entire leadership teams. Others dispatched pastors to *"go see what God is doing."* No social media existed. No marketing campaign promoted the meetings. Word of mouth alone fuelled what soon became a global pilgrimage.

A revival unlike others

The Toronto Blessing differed from historical revivals in several ways. It was not centred on mass evangelism, as with Billy Graham crusades. It was not defined by fiery preaching like the Welsh Revival (1904) or the Great Awakenings. Nor was it linked to dramatic social transformation, though it influenced many communities indirectly.

Instead, this movement was marked by personal renewal - deep emotional healing, release from shame, restoration of joy, and encounters with the Holy Spirit that reshaped people from the inside out. Many described it as being *"filled with the Father's love."*

The most common testimonies involved the transformation of marriages, overcoming of long-held wounds, new boldness in ministry, and a profound hunger for Scripture and prayer.

Leaders repeatedly emphasised that the manifestations were not the point. The heart of the movement was intimacy with God, freedom through the Spirit, and a renewed passion for Jesus. The laughter, tears, shaking, or falling were simply responses to a deep work happening beneath the surface.

Theological anchors amid experience

Though critics accused the movement of excess, emotionalism, or lack of theological clarity, the leadership consistently pointed to Scripture to frame what was happening.

Passages frequently cited included:

- *"The joy of the Lord is your strength"* (Nehemiah 8:10)
- *"In your presence there is fullness of joy"* (Psalm 16:11)
- *"Be filled with the Spirit"* (Ephesians 5:18)
- *"The Spirit himself testifies with our spirit that we are God's children"* (Romans 8:16)
- *"Times of refreshing... from the Lord"* (Acts 3:19)

Their message was simple: if the Holy Spirit fills people today as He did in Acts, if the presence of God brings joy and freedom, and if the Father desires to pour His love into hearts, then encounters that reflect these realities should not surprise us. This grounding in Scripture helped shape a movement that valued both experience and truth. While not every expression was perfect - and leaders occasionally intervened to bring correction - the overall emphasis remained on Christ, His love, His presence, and His power to heal.

The global spread of renewal

Within the first two years, more than 300,000 visitors travelled to Toronto. Entire denominations sent official delegations to witness the meetings. Conferences multiplied. Many who visited returned home forever altered.

- In the **United Kingdom**, Anglican churches experienced significant renewal, culminating in the rapid expansion of the Alpha Course as a tool for evangelism and Spirit-filled discipleship.

- In **South Africa**, churches across denominational lines reported powerful encounters leading to unity, reconciliation, and healing in the post-apartheid era.

- In **Australia and New Zealand**, prayer movements, worship ministries, and mission initiatives sprang up with fresh energy.

- In **Scandinavia**, pastors and young leaders carried renewal fire back to their congregations, shaping worship culture for decades.

- In **Asia**, especially in South Korea and Malaysia, visitors from Toronto helped catalyse prayer networks and outreach ministries.

It would be impossible to quantify the full global impact. Songs written in the wake of Toronto found their way into churches worldwide. Leaders who were renewed launched church plants, missionary organisations, inner healing ministries, and worship training schools. Even sceptics acknowledged that thousands of lives were genuinely changed.

The Father's love: A central theme

More than anything, Toronto became associated with the clear message of the Father's love. Many Christians - despite years of faithful church involvement - carried some very deep wounds from rejection, fear, legalism, or religious striving. They believed God loved them in theory but struggled to live in that reality.

Toronto changed that for multitudes. Attendees testified that for the first time they felt *safe* in God's presence. They felt *wanted*, not tolerated. They felt *embraced*, not merely forgiven. The parable of the prodigal son (Luke 15) became the interpretive lens through which many understood their experience— returning home to a Father who ran to them, embraced them, and restored them.

This emphasis on the Father-heart of God became perhaps Toronto's greatest legacy. Dozens of ministries founded in its wake built their identity around helping believers discover emotional and spiritual wholeness through the love of God.

Critique, controversy, and discernment

As with every revival, Toronto was not without its critics. Some were very concerned about rather unusual manifestations. Others questioned theological precision. Some feared emotional excess or a serious lack of oversight. Leaders acknowledged these concerns and offered repeated teaching on testing the spirits, evaluating fruit, and grounding experience in Scripture.

Nevertheless, criticism could not mute the testimonies. Pastors reported healed marriages, reconciled relationships, restored ministries, and churches revitalised by renewed prayer, unity, and compassion. While some dismissed the movement, others recognised that God often works through the unpredictable, the surprising, and the uncomfortable.

The beginning of a larger story

The Toronto Blessing did not exist in isolation. It became one of the key catalysts for what many scholars later called the global charismatic renewal of the late 20th and early 21st centuries. Its DNA can be traced in:

- the rise of global worship movements
- the expansion of ministry training schools
- the growth of healing and prophetic ministries
- the strengthening of intercession networks
- the planting of thousands of churches worldwide

Its influence is not fading; it continues to shape the leadership of whole denominations, ministries, missionary organisations, and worship communities around the world.

The story of Toronto is the story of what God can do with a small group of hungry people who simply create space for Him to move. It is the story of how one unexpected night can become the spark that ignites fires across nations. It is also a story that invites every generation to remain open, humble, prayerful, and expectant - as the God who moved in 1994 is the same God moving today.

The global spread

What began in a modest auditorium near Toronto's Pearson Airport in early 1994 quickly grew into one of the most globally influential renewal movements of the late twentieth century. By the end of its first year, the *Toronto Blessing* had become a phrase recognised not only in North America but throughout Europe, Africa, Asia, Oceania, and Latin America.

The scale of its spread was unprecedented: visitors returned home transformed, and testimonies produced expectation that God might do in their cities what He was doing in Canada. Word travelled through churches, missionary networks, conferences, cassette tapes, newsletters, prayer circles, and charismatic communities hungry for fresh wind from the Spirit.

From local renewal to global pilgrimage

Within weeks of the initial outpouring, pastors and believers from across North America began visiting Toronto. Some came out of curiosity, some out of desperation, some in scepticism, and others with hearts already primed by prayer for revival. What they encountered there - extended worship, ministry times that stretched late into the night, physical and emotional healing, deep repentance, and an overwhelming sense of God's Fatherly love - often upended their expectations.

This produced a unique phenomenon: Toronto became a global pilgrimage site. Unlike Azusa Street in 1906, where international visitors were relatively few, Toronto emerged in an age when international travel was more accessible and charismatic networks more extensive.

Pastors from the United States, the United Kingdom, South Korea, Brazil, Australia, New Zealand, Singapore, South Africa, Nigeria, and many others travelled to the meetings.

It was not uncommon for visiting leaders to stay for multiple days, attending afternoon teachings, evening services, and late-night ministry sessions. Many said they were "undone" by the palpable nearness of God. They returned home carrying what they believed to be "a fire" to share with their congregations.

In Scripture, such moments of divine encounter often led to mission impact. Moses at the burning bush (Exodus 3:1-6), Isaiah's temple encounter (Isaiah 6:1-8), or the apostles at Pentecost in Acts 2. Encounter becomes empowerment. Toronto functioned similarly: the experience sent people out.

The United Kingdom: Revival embers ignite

Among the nations most affected was the United Kingdom. Within months of the first visitors returning, reports of similar renewal began surfacing across England, Scotland, Wales, and Northern Ireland. churches as diverse as Anglican, Baptist, Pentecostal, Vineyard, Newfrontiers, and various independent charismatic congregations described meetings marked by exuberant worship, extended ministry, bursts of laughter, tears of repentance, shaking, falling, and profound emotional healing. For many leaders, it was the first time their churches had seen such sustained hunger for the Spirit. Mid-week services were packed. Prayer lines stretched across sanctuaries. Evangelistic openness rose dramatically as believers shared testimonies with friends and family.

Notably, Holy Trinity Brompton (HTB) - future birthplace of the global Alpha Course movement - experienced dramatic renewal shortly after its leaders visited Toronto. This would later shape the worship style, ministry atmosphere, and evangelistic DNA of one of the most influential churches in the world.

The UK renewal created a deep ripple effect right across Europe. Scandinavian churches hosted extended meetings. Germany saw a fresh wave of charismatic expression. In France, Belgium, the Netherlands, and Switzerland, pastors reported new signs of spiritual hunger. Even historically conservative denominations quietly acknowledged that the Spirit seemed to be stirring something unusual.

South Africa and Sub-Saharan Africa: A fresh wind

When South African pastors who visited Toronto returned home, they found their congregations eager for renewal. Meetings in Cape Town, Johannesburg, Durban, and Pretoria began to attract people seeking healing, reconciliation, and a deeper awareness of God's presence - particularly powerful in the years following the end of apartheid. Elsewhere in Africa, such as Uganda, Kenya, Nigeria, and Ghana, Toronto's influence mixed with pre-existing revival traditions.

African churches already understood spiritual power, and deliverance, and worship expressed with joy. Toronto added a dimension of emotional healing and the assurance of the Father's love, which resonated deeply in communities scarred by conflict or poverty.

Asia and Oceania: Silence breaks into renewal

In South Korea, Singapore, Malaysia, and parts of China, pastors returning from Toronto began holding renewal meetings that sometimes lasted through the night. Korean prayer culture, already intense and fervent, blended naturally with Toronto-style ministry. The result was a deeply emotional experience, marked by tears, repentance, and strong prophetic expression.

In Australia and New Zealand, meetings associated with the Toronto revival filled churches for months. Some pastors described it as *"a warm wave washing through the nation,"* particularly among younger believers who encountered the Spirit's power in ways they had never previously known.

The Americas beyond Toronto

In the United States, Toronto's influence intersected with several existing renewal streams. Some churches embraced this new move wholeheartedly; others approached it cautiously. The Vineyard movement itself eventually distanced from the Toronto church, preferring a more regulated approach to such manifestations.

Yet outside the denominational boundaries, Toronto's influence spread widely. Large conferences and mission gatherings drew thousands who were eager to experience renewal.

In Latin America, particularly Brazil, Argentina, and Chile, Toronto blended with local evangelical and several Pentecostal traditions already marked by revival. Emotional expression, healing ministry, and prophetic worship were not new - but the Toronto emphasis on relational healing and the Father's love brought fresh depth.

Renewal through worship

One of the most enduring legacies of the Toronto Blessing is its impact on contemporary worship across the world. The renewal birthed hundreds of songs - simple, intimate, focused on the Father's heart. The worship style emphasised soaking in God's presence, waiting on Him, and responding spontaneously rather than "performing" songs.

Many churches across the world adopted Toronto-style worship, influencing later movements such as Vineyard Music, Hillsong Worship, Jesus Culture, IHOP-KC, and countless independent worship communities.

The Psalms capture this posture beautifully:

"In Your presence there is fullness of joy." (Psalm 16:11).

"My heart says of You, 'Seek His face!' Your face, LORD, I will seek." (Psalm 27:8).

Toronto worship was not about entertainment - it was all about encountering God.

The Father's love: A message that travelled far

More than laughter, falling, or any outward manifestation, the core message of the Toronto Blessing was the unconditional love of the Father. For many decades, large segments of the church emphasised the holiness of God, the sovereignty of God, or the mission of God. Toronto reintroduced believers to the tenderness of God.

Everywhere the renewal spread, testimonies emerged:

- Pastors healed of burnout and resentment
- believers freed from shame or father-wounds
- marriages restored
- prodigals returning
- missionaries renewed in their calling

This was not superficial emotionalism. Many attendees said it was the deepest moment of healing they had ever experienced.

Controversy, discernment, and the search for balance

As with every major revival in Christian history, the Toronto Blessing generated controversy. Some leaders questioned the physical manifestations. Others worried about imbalance or lack of theological teaching. Still others felt that human excess sometimes overshadowed genuine spiritual work. These deep concerns were not without merit. Toronto, like Azusa Street, the Welsh Revival, and even early Methodist revivalism, required wise pastoral oversight. Yet despite criticism, the scriptural truth remained: *"Do not treat prophecies with contempt but test them all; hold on to what is good."* (1 Thessalonians 5:20–21). The church was invited not to reject the movement wholesale, but to discern its fruit - and the fruit was significant and lasting.

A renewal that reached the generations

One of the most surprising effects of the Toronto Blessing was its long-term generational impact. Many leaders who visited Toronto in the 1990s have, over the past three decades, shaped global worship, missions, church-planting, youth ministry, and evangelism. Even young children touched in those early meetings often grew into adults with deep spiritual sensitivity and vibrant faith.

This generational aspect explains why Toronto's influence remains visible even today - not because people still pursue the manifestations, but because many of today's leaders were formed in the atmosphere of renewal.

As the Toronto Blessing matured beyond those explosive early months, its influence began to take on a more defined and lasting form. What began as nightly meetings in a modest building near an airport evolved into a multi-stream river of renewal that touched denominations, leadership development, worship culture, missions, and the global prayer movement. While the initial manifestations attracted the most attention - both positive and critical - the enduring effects would be found not primarily in manifestations, but in *transformation*.

Lives changed, ministries were birthed, churches were renewed, and leaders were completely reshaped: these became the true legacy of Toronto.

A new language of worship

Few movements in recent church history have influenced worship as profoundly as the Toronto Blessing. During the mid-1990s and into the early 2000s, worship emerging from the movement contributed significantly to the global charismatic and evangelical liturgy. The emphasis on intimacy with God - particularly God as Father - reshaped the worship vocabulary around the world. Songs that spoke of God's embrace, His nearness, His healing love, and His delight in His children became central.

This shift was more than sentimental. For many believers, Toronto helped dismantle deeply rooted fears of God's rejection or disapproval. People who had lived under condemnation or shame began to sing openly about grace, acceptance, and joy. This became a theological corrective for believers who, though orthodox in creed, had lived emotionally distant from God. The movement's worship style - simple, repetitive, heart-focused, open to the Spirit - reflected the Psalmist's longing: *"One thing I ask from the Lord… that I may dwell in the house of the Lord all the days of my life."* (Psalm 27:4).

These worship patterns in time influenced countless churches worldwide. Worship teams visited Toronto, returned home with fresh fire, and began writing or adapting songs. The global worship landscape, already shifting through movements like Vineyard Music and later Hillsong, found in Toronto an infusion of intimacy and prophetic spontaneity.

Even today, many worship leaders can trace their personal awakening back to experiences in Toronto or conferences which were influenced by that movement. I am one of those people. I met John and Carol Arnott when they came to Australia. I was able to speak with them about what really happened that night in Toronto back in 1994.

I will never forget our chat. It was in 1996 and the whole world had been turned upside down following the events in their Church and yet I was profoundly moved by the simplicity and the humility of these two very normal, everyday believers, who were just as surprised as the rest of the world when God showed up in such a demonstrable way in what was a normal service.

We spoke about the excesses and the counterfeit and the work of the enemy to deceive and John and Carol were not defensive in any way. They had nothing to defend, because they didn't do anything to trigger this amazing movement. They just had to try and pastor the people whose lives were completely changed because of what God had done.

I had seen the flow on effect of Toronto in the church I was pastoring at the time, and I have no doubt to this day, that God was in the midst of this worldwide phenomenon.

Healing the wounded heart

Perhaps the most enduring theological contribution of the Toronto Blessing is its emphasis on inner healing - particularly healing from trauma, family wounds, pastoral burnout, and spiritual exhaustion. Many Christians arrived in Toronto broken, discouraged, or carrying emotional pain that had never been addressed in traditional church settings. They encountered a ministry environment where healing prayer, forgiveness, emotional honesty, and the Father's love were at the centre.

Testimony after testimony from the mid-1990s through the early 2000s showed patterns of emotional and relational restoration:

- pastors restored after burnout
- couples healed after years of distance
- believers freed from lifelong shame
- individuals delivered from burdens of legalism
- missionaries renewed after trauma
- young adults discovering identity and purpose in Christ

This emphasis on healing was not new to the Christian tradition, but Toronto brought it to the forefront of church life on a global scale. It reminded the church that evangelism and discipleship cannot flourish when believers carry deep, unaddressed wounds. Jesus' ministry, after all, included healing the broken-hearted (Luke 4:18), and revival history consistently shows that renewal often begins with inner restoration.

This focus on emotional and spiritual healing subsequently inspired numerous ministries, seminars, and global conferences. While some models needed refinement over time, the core insight - that God heals the whole person, not only the intellect - remains a key legacy of Toronto.

A theology of joy and the renewal of the imagination

One of the most controversial features of the Toronto Blessing was the manifestation of joy—sometimes expressed through laughter, shaking, falling, or tears. While critics questioned whether such experiences were appropriate or biblical, supporters pointed to the often-overlooked biblical theme of joy in encounters with God. *"In your presence there is fullness of joy."* (Psalm 16:11). The Spirit's fruit includes joy (Galatians 5:22). The early church experienced awe and gladness (Acts 2:46-47).

The movement's distinctive was not the physical manifestations themselves, but the theological correction beneath them: joy is not optional in the Christian life; it is central. Many believers who had lived under heavy burdens or strict religious environments found liberation in joy. For some, laughter became a physical release from emotional oppression. For others, joy restored their imagination, reviving hope, creativity, and spiritual expectation.

Over time, pastors who once approached God with trepidation or duty began approaching Him with delight. churches historically marked by formality rediscovered spontaneity. Worship, prayer, and preaching regained their vibrancy. While debates continue about how these manifestations should be interpreted, few deny that Toronto played a significant role in re-awakening the church to the spiritual gift of joy.

Global missions impact: Fire spreading outward

One of the least recognised and yet most important fruits of the Toronto Blessing is its long-term impact on global missions. The renewal did not remain confined to worship gatherings; it birthed mission sending, evangelistic passion, and many new ministries across the world.

Many missionaries who visited Toronto returned to their fields with fresh boldness, renewed intimacy with God, and greater resilience. Testimonies abound of mission teams experiencing breakthrough after receiving ministry in Toronto.

Multiple mission organisations trace significant growth to those renewal years. Churches that once viewed missions as just a peripheral responsibility began prioritising it with a passion. Short-term and long-term mission projects increased rapidly. Evangelistic healings, profound prophetic ministry, and prayer mobilisation intensified, especially in those regions resistant to traditional approaches.

This pattern echoes the book of Acts, where encounters with the Holy Spirit were consistently followed by expansion of the gospel. Toronto's emphasis on empowerment and intimacy helped reshape the missionary identity from burden-bearing servants to beloved sons and daughters carrying the Father's heart into the nations.

Leadership renewal and the healing of Pastors

A lesser known but vital dimension of Toronto's legacy is the renewal of Christian leaders. Pastors, missionaries, and ministry workers arrived exhausted, wounded, or on the edge of quitting. Many said Toronto saved their ministries - and in some cases, their lives.

Leadership renewal came through:

- extended times of personal prayer and worship
- healing of leadership wounds

- prophetic encouragement
- reconnection with calling
- restoration of joy
- release from fear of failure
- new humility and authenticity in ministry

Leaders learned that ministry must flow from intimacy, not performance. This core insight reshaped pastoral practice across many denominations. Conferences and retreats inspired by the renewal continue to offer safe spaces for leaders to encounter God without pressure to perform.

Critique and correction: A mature legacy

No revival is without its imperfections. Toronto faced criticism from within evangelical, charismatic, and traditional circles. Concerns included excess emotionalism, insufficient theological grounding, and a lack of oversight for unusual manifestations. Some individuals or churches adopted practices that needed correction. The Vineyard movement, which originally covered the church, eventually distanced itself due to their theological concerns about the emphasis and direction.

These critiques were painful but important. They forced leaders to refine their theology, strengthen accountability structures, and place renewed emphasis on scriptural grounding. Over time, the balanced teaching of God's love, the centrality of Scripture, and the lordship of Christ helped the movement mature. The lasting fruit is found not in extremes, but in this mature, refined legacy.

The enduring legacy

Today, the church that hosted the renewal - now called *Catch the Fire Toronto* - continues to thrive as a hub for worship, healing, and global mission. The wider Catch the Fire network spans multiple nations, carrying a distinct emphasis on the Father's love, the person and power of the Holy Spirit, and the healing of the heart. Many leaders in the contemporary charismatic world trace their spiritual formation to the Toronto years.

More broadly, the Toronto Blessing shaped an entire generation. It influenced worship, prayer movements, healing ministries, discipleship approaches, and missions strategies. It revived spiritual hunger at a time when many believed revival was impossible in the modern West.

Most importantly, Toronto reintroduced the global church to the Father's heart - to a God who not only saves but embraces; who not only forgives but delights in His children; who not only calls but empowers.

11. THE BROWNSVILLE REVIVAL (1995–2000): A NATION STIRRED

On Father's Day, Sunday 18th June 1995, in the heart of the American South, events unfolded in the Brownsville Assembly of God church in Pensacola, Florida, that would reshape the spiritual landscape of the United States for years to come. The congregation had been praying intensely for revival - two and a half years of Tuesday-night meetings devoted almost entirely to intercession. Their pastor, John Kilpatrick, had led the church through a sustained season of longing, urging them to cry out for the renewed presence of God. The prayer *"Lord, send revival to Brownsville"* had become more than a slogan. It was a desperate plea rooted in Isaiah's cry: *"Oh, that you would rend the heavens and come down."* (Isaiah 64:1).

That particular morning had felt quite ordinary in every external sense. The sanctuary was full, visitors had come for Father's Day, and evangelist Steve Hill - recently touched in a fresh outpouring at Holy Trinity Brompton in London – was invited to preach. No one expected anything unusual. And yet, what unfolded after Hill's message lit a fire that burned for five years, drew over four million people to a local church campus, and became one of the most dynamic and significant revival movements in modern American history.

The spark that ignited Brownsville

Eyewitness accounts describe a moment early in the ministry time when the presence of God seemed to descend with unusual weight. People began to rush to the altar, many falling to their knees in repentance before Hill even issued an invitation. Children and adults alike began to weep openly. Long-standing believers cried out for God's mercy. Entire families gathered at the front, praying together. The sound of intercession filled the room - not choreographed, not manipulated, but spontaneous. Pastor Kilpatrick, who had been deeply exhausted from years of pastoral burdens, later recounted that he felt the power of God surge through him in a way he had never known.

He collapsed on the platform - not out of emotional disturbance, but under what he described as *"a holy weight, like liquid love washing over me."* For the next several hours, the congregation remained in a posture of utter brokenness and surrender. Many stayed long after the official meeting ended, reluctant to leave the sanctuary.

Something had undeniably changed. When the church gathered the next evening, the crowds were larger. More repentance. More tears. More unmistakable signs of God's presence. Within days, the story had spread across Pensacola. Within weeks, people were travelling from neighbouring states. Within months, the Brownsville Revival had become a national phenomenon.

A revival marked by repentance

Unlike Toronto's emphasis on personal renewal and the Father's love, Brownsville's signature theme was repentance. Not superficial regret, but deep, Spirit-born conviction. People testified that the holiness of God felt tangible, almost luminous in the room, exposing sin yet offering mercy. The *cry "Jesus, forgive me"* became the soundtrack of the revival.

Every night - six nights a week for years - the altars filled within minutes of the sermon's conclusion. Steve Hill's evangelistic preaching was direct, urgent, and confrontational, echoing the boldness of John the Baptist or the fervency of the Wesleyan awakenings. He preached Christ crucified, sin confronted, grace extended, and transformation demanded. Many thousands came forward, including drug dealers, teenagers, businessmen, backslidden Christians, nominal churchgoers, , pastors, atheists. Some collapsed in sobs. Some shook under conviction. Others stood silently, overwhelmed.

This focus on repentance set Brownsville apart from many contemporary movements. Worship was passionate, emotional, and loud, driven by the music of Lindell Cooley, whose songs such as *"Mercy Seat"* and *"Look What the Lord Has Done"* became anthems of the revival. But at the centre was always the altar - a place where brokenness, forgiveness, and new beginnings met.

Why repentance captured a generation

The 1990s in America were marked by cultural shifts: rising teen drug use, the aftermath of the moral turbulence of the 1980s, a spike in broken families, and a growing sense that Christian faith was sliding toward social irrelevance. For many young people, the message of Brownsville hit a nerve. They were hungry for authenticity, holiness, and purpose in life. This revival offered a Christianity that demanded something of them - a call to radical surrender rather than cultural accommodation.

Night after night, young people poured into the sanctuary. Many described feeling "a fire" run through them, a burning desire to follow Jesus completely. Bold testimonies of deliverance from addiction, self-harm, and occult involvement became common. One moment captured by news crews showed a line of over a thousand teenagers waiting outside several hours before the doors opened - holding Bibles, singing worship songs, praying for friends. It resembled not a concert queue, but a spiritual pilgrimage.

Brownsville's emphasis on holiness resonated deeply: *"Be holy, because I am holy."* (1 Peter 1:16). Yet the holiness preached was not legalistic. It was relational - a longing to belong to Christ completely, body, mind, and heart.

The atmosphere of the meetings

Visitors routinely described the atmosphere of the revival as electric, weighty, and saturated with expectation. From the moment people entered the building, they sensed a seriousness about the things of God. Ushers often prayed for people before they found their seats. Worship erupted with dancing, shouting, clapping, tears. Cooley's worship team led with great joy and reverence combined.

But the hallmark was always the preaching of the Word and the altar. Sermons were fiery yet grounded in Scripture. The call to repentance was unashamed. And when the invitation came, hundreds moved instantly, sometimes even before words were spoken.

The altar ministry team - comprising trained volunteers - prayed with thousands nightly. Deliverance occurred regularly. People testified to physical healings, reconciliation of marriages, and lifelong bondages breaking.

What made Brownsville unique was not emotionalism but the consistent fruit of changed lives. Local newspapers, secular journalists, and even sceptical observers noted the transformation of the city: crime dropping, church attendance increasing, and countless testimonies of restored families.

The role of intercessory prayer

Behind the visible revival lay a furnace of prayer. The Tuesday-night intercessions that preceded 1995 continued throughout the revival's duration. Intercessors met for hours, praying for the lost, for the nation, for the local church, for purity among leaders, and for protection amid criticism.

Many described sensing spiritual warfare more acutely during these years. Pensacola became, in the eyes of the intercessors, a battleground where forces of darkness were being challenged. Their prayers reflected Ephesians 6:12: *"For our struggle is not against flesh and blood..."* Intercession became not a supplement to the revival but a sustaining pillar. Without it, leaders believed, the movement would have collapsed under its own weight.

If the opening months of the Brownsville Revival were marked by surprise, conviction, and overwhelming hunger for God, the years that followed revealed something even more significant: a sustained move of the Holy Spirit that reordered lives, reshaped families, revitalised churches, and sent waves of renewal across the United States and beyond. Unlike many revivals that flash brightly and fade quickly, Brownsville displayed an unusual endurance.

Night after night, for years, people travelled from around the world - many waiting for hours under the humid Florida sun - to experience what God was doing. It became one of the longest-running local church revivals in modern American history.

A church transformed from the inside out

Brownsville Assembly of God in Pensacola did not simply host revival meetings; the revival remade the church from within. Before Father's Day 1995, it had been a very solid congregation, burdened by a sense of spiritual dryness. After revival broke out, the congregation found itself at the centre of a global spiritual phenomenon. Attendance soared from 2,000 to thousands more. Ushers multiplied. Prayer teams expanded. Nursery ministries, hospitality ministries, and counselling rooms all had to be established quickly to meet the overwhelming need.

The revival required the congregation to mature rapidly. They needed humility, flexibility, and a willingness to make room for the unexpected. Pastors later testified how the revival changed them as much as it changed visitors. Many church members described their experience in similar terms: they became more prayerful, more compassionate, more courageous in evangelism, more devoted to Scripture.

This transformation reflected the New Testament pattern: when the Spirit moves, the church grows in holiness and mission. In Acts, the early Christian community was marked by devotion - *"They devoted themselves to the apostles' teaching and to fellowship, to the breaking of bread and to prayer."* (Acts 2:42). Something similar unfolded in Brownsville. What began as a visitation became discipleship.

Conviction, repentance, and the power of God

Although Brownsville came to be known for its intensity - loud worship, strong preaching, visible emotion - the core of the revival was not noise but repentance. Night after night, the altar filled with people sobbing, kneeling, repenting, and crying out for the mercy of God. This emphasis on repentance became one of the defining characteristics of the movement. Steve Hill's preaching played a central role. His messages were urgent but not manipulative, passionate but grounded in Scripture. He spoke of sin, salvation, holiness, and the blood of Jesus with clarity and conviction.

He preached Christ crucified and risen, calling people to *"run to the cross."* The message was very simple and uncompromising: salvation is found in Christ alone, and repentance is the fruit. Visitors testified that they felt "arrested" by the presence of God the moment they simply stepped onto the property. Others said conviction hit them before the sermon even began. Some recounted that they tried to stay in their seats during the altar call but felt compelled to respond. Repentance was not a side-element - it was the heart of the revival.

This aligns with the biblical promise: *"When he comes, he will prove the world to be in the wrong about sin and righteousness and judgment."* (John 16:8). The Spirit's work of conviction was unmistakable at Brownsville. It produced changed lives, reconciled marriages, restored prodigals, and a generation of young people marked by seriousness about holiness.

The worship that became a soundtrack of revival

Music played an enormous role in Brownsville's atmosphere. Worship leaders Lindell Cooley and later others carried the meetings with a sound that blended passionate praise, heartfelt longing, and spiritual warfare. Songs like *"Refiner's Fire," "I Need You More," "Enemy's Camp," "Look What the Lord Has Done,"* and *"The Spirit of the Sovereign Lord"* became anthems.

The worship was not entertainment - it was a divine encounter. It prepared hearts for the Word and softened resistance so people could receive what the Spirit wanted to do. Cooley once said, "Our job was to help people look at Jesus." And that's exactly what happened. The music was simple, repetitive at times, but saturated with longing: longing for holiness, longing for purity, longing for God's presence. Long stretches of worship created a sense of expectation. People often arrived hours early, and worship began before the official service started. The presence of God came before the preaching, sometimes before the first song even began. Many testified that they had never experienced worship like Brownsville's - raw, unpolished, wholehearted. It captured the essence of Psalm 22:3: *"You are enthroned as the Holy One; you are the one Israel praises."*

A generation marked for mission

One of the most significant outcomes of the revival was how it touched young people. Teens and young adults came in buses, vans, and caravans. Some arrived rebellious, apathetic, or addicted. Many left transformed.

In response to this wave, the Brownsville School of Ministry (B.S.M.) was founded in 1997 under the leadership of Dr. Michael Brown. The school focused on holiness, Scripture, prayer, and evangelism. Thousands applied. Students came from dozens of nations, hungry to be equipped for ministry. The school quickly gained a reputation for rigorous discipleship and theological depth paired with spiritual passion.

Many graduates today serve as pastors, church planters, missionaries, evangelists, and worship leaders right around the world. Brownsville's impact on global mission can never be overstated: it launched a generation into the harvest fields. Jesus' words seemed to echo through the corridors of the school: *"The harvest is plentiful but the workers are few."* (Matthew 9:37). Brownsville helped raise workers for that harvest.

Miracles, deliverance, and the reality of spiritual warfare

Although Brownsville did not emphasise manifestations to the degree seen in Toronto, supernatural moments were common. Healings occurred, sometimes quietly, sometimes dramatically. People testified to deliverance from addiction, depression, and spiritual oppression. Prayer teams ministered deep emotional healing to those burdened by trauma or sin.

The church took these things very seriously. They did not sensationalise. They counselled, discipled, and taught. They emphasised Scripture and pastoral care. They understood that spiritual warfare was real but that the answer was Jesus, not theatrics. The revival challenged many churches to consider again Paul's reminder: *"Our struggle is not against flesh and blood."* (Ephesians 6:12). Brownsville reminded the American church that the supernatural realm is not theoretical but actual.

Criticism, controversy, and the cost of revival

No major revival in history escapes scrutiny, and Brownsville was no exception. Critics questioned all the emotionalism, the longevity of the meetings, the use of catchers, the intensity of the altar calls, even the sincerity of the repentance. Others raised concerns about finances, theology, or pastoral burnout.

Such criticism was certainly not new; the Great Awakenings, The Welsh Revival, Azusa Street, and Toronto all faced similar responses. Revival by nature challenges comfort and exposes hearts; it can divide as well as unite.

Brownsville leaders acknowledged shortcomings. They later said they wished they had strengthened pastoral structures earlier, managed the schedule more sustainably, and cultivated better long-term rhythms. But they never doubted that God had moved. Even critics agreed the fruit was undeniable: lives changed, marriages restored, addictions broken, thousands saved.

Revival brings blessing - but also cost. For Brownsville, that cost included total exhaustion, high pressure, misunderstanding, and eventually the natural slowing and closing of the revival season. But even as the nightly meetings ceased, the impact remained.

A fire that still burns

Today, Brownsville continues to influence pastors, worship leaders, intercessors, and evangelists who experienced it firsthand. Its sound, its messages, its emphasis on repentance and holiness still shape churches across denominations. It demonstrated that even in a culture drifting far from God, the Holy Spirit can come with conviction and power. For many, Brownsville made revival something tangible - not just a story from past centuries, but a lived reality. What happened at Brownsville was never intended to remain inside the walls of a single congregation on the western edge of Pensacola. From the earliest days, Steve Hill declared that revival loses its purpose if it does not lead to mission.

The meetings were not an end in themselves but a launching pad. Night after night, Hill pleaded with believers to *"win the lost at any cost,"* echoing the apostolic heartbeat of the early church. This missionary impulse became one of Brownsville's lasting legacies, transforming the revival from a local movement into a national and global catalyst.

A new generation of evangelists

One of the most striking outcomes of Brownsville was the sheer number of evangelists raised up during this period. As the revival progressed, thousands of young people, many of whom had never imagined themselves preaching, sensed a call to evangelism. Some came from broken backgrounds; others were church-raised but spiritually lukewarm. Under the intense conviction and empowerment of the Spirit, many surrendered their lives to full-time ministry.

Over time, hundreds of graduates from the Brownsville Revival School of Ministry (BRSM) moved into cities, towns, and nations with a burden to preach the gospel. Some became pastors and church planters; others became itinerant evangelists. Many of them cite Brownsville as the place where their spiritual eyes opened - where holiness became non-negotiable, where prayer became central, and where evangelism became their life's call.

Their ministries have since touched nations throughout Africa, Latin America, Europe, and Asia. Though the revival meetings themselves ended in 2000, their evangelistic impact continues in these lives - a testament to what happens when revival flows outward and not merely upward.

The impact on worship and prayer

Brownsville also produced a worship sound that later shaped countless churches around the world. Lindell Cooley, the worship pastor during the revival, helped usher in a new era of revival worship marked by simplicity, intensity, and heartfelt longing for God. Songs such as *"I Need You More,"* *"Healing Waters,"* *"Freedom,"* and *"Rain Down"* became part of the worship vocabulary of congregations far beyond Pensacola.

These songs were not written to entertain; they were birthed in an atmosphere where the presence of God felt weighty and tangible. Worship during the revival often lasted for extensive periods, becoming a place of surrender, repentance, and joy. People did not simply sing — they wept, knelt, danced, rejoiced, and prayed. The sanctuary became an altar, and worship became the language of transformed hearts.

Equally important was the revival's effect on prayer. Before the outpouring began, Brownsville was known for its intercessory prayer culture under the leadership of Pastor Kilpatrick. Once the revival started, prayer deepened further. Intercessors met for hours before services. Prayer lines formed long before worship began. Thousands arrived early simply to kneel and seek God.

This prayer movement became one of the revival's pillars, reinforcing the truth that revival is not sustained by emotional momentum but by intercessory perseverance. Many prayer ministries worldwide later credited Brownsville as a model for corporate crying-out to God.

Youth and the great wave of repentance

Among all the demographic groups touched by Brownsville, none responded more dramatically than young people. Youth groups travelled to Pensacola by the bus-load. Thousands of teenagers flooded the altars night after night, confessing hidden sin, renouncing destructive lifestyles, making restitution with families, and surrendering their lives to Christ.

An entire generation can now remember waiting for hours in the sweltering Florida heat simply to enter the building. They were not coerced. They were not bribed. They were not manipulated. They came because they sensed God was real and calling them.

Many of these young people returned home transformed. In some cities, youth revivals broke out in schools and churches after groups came back from Brownsville. Prayer meetings started spontaneously. Testimonies spread. Families were restored. Entire youth ministries changed direction.

This youth awakening forms one of Brownsville's most undeniable fruits. While critics often focused on the revival's manifestations, historians now note that the moral and missional transformation among young people remains one of the revival's strongest evidences of authenticity.

Global visitors and international ripples

Though Brownsville was a local church, the world came to it. Week after week, nations were represented in the sanctuary. Many travelled from the UK, Brazil, South Korea, South Africa, Sweden, Germany, Australia, and multiple other regions.

Some came because they were desperate for renewal in their own ministries. Others came because they heard rumours of awakening and wanted to see for themselves. Still others came as sceptics, only to encounter God unexpectedly.

International leaders who visited often returned home transformed. In some nations, revival meetings ignited after pastors shared what they had experienced in Pensacola. In others, Brownsville's emphasis on holiness, evangelism, and prayer, reshaped congregational life. Several churches began 24-hour prayer cycles. Others launched street-evangelism teams. A few even developed Bible schools modelled on BRSM.

This world-wide influence helps explain why Brownsville is remembered not only as a local revival but as a movement that reverberated far beyond the borders of the United States.

Balancing testimony and tension

No revival is without its tensions or controversies, and Brownsville was no exception. Every major awakening in history has carried a mixture of divine fire and human frailty.

Some critics argued that the manifestations - shaking, weeping, falling under God's power - were excessive. Others questioned the sustainability of nightly meetings or the emotional toll on leaders.

Yet, despite these concerns, the widespread testimony of transformed lives remains difficult to dismiss. People were saved. Families were healed. Addictions were broken. Evangelists were called. churches were renewed. Whenever the history of Brownsville is discussed, even critics often acknowledge the depth of repentance and the authenticity of many changed lives.

As with the First Great Awakening, the Welsh Revival, Azusa Street, or Toronto, the church must learn to discern both the gold and the impurities - honouring what God did while also acknowledging the human limitations within any movement.

Why Brownsville still matters today

Though the nightly meetings ceased long ago, the revival's message remains potent for the contemporary church:

- *Holiness is essential*, not optional. Revival begins where repentance is taken seriously.
- *Evangelism must flow out of revival*, not wait for it.
- *Prayer is the engine*, not the afterthought, of renewal.
- *Youth hunger for truth*, not entertainment.
- *The presence of God transforms*, beyond what programs or strategies can accomplish.

In an age of distraction, spiritual apathy, and cultural upheaval, Brownsville serves as a reminder that God still responds to desperate prayer and repentant hearts. The revival's greatest contribution may not be its manifestations or its meetings, but the renewed conviction that God is holy, God is merciful, and God is willing to awaken nations when His people seek Him.

The chapter closes - but the fire continues

By the time the Brownsville Revival concluded in the early 2000s, millions had been touched in some way by its influence - directly or indirectly. Its legacy continues through all the churches planted, the ministers trained, the mission fields reached, and the tens of thousands of believers awakened.

Though the lights dimmed on that particular season, the fire has never fully gone out. It burns in the lives of those who met Christ powerfully in Pensacola, in the ministries birthed from its altar, and in the global church's memory.

The question Brownsville leaves with us is simple but searching: If God were to pour out His Spirit again with such power, would we be ready - and willing - to respond?

12. THE SMITHTON/SPRINGFIELD OUTPOURING (1996–2005): SMALL TOWN, GLOBAL IMPACT

On a very quiet Sunday evening in March 1996, in the small rural community of Smithton, Missouri - population barely 500 - a local congregation experienced what would later be recognised as one of the most surprising and far-reaching American revival movements of the late 20th and early 21st centuries.

The church, Smithton Community church, pastored by Steve and Kathy Gray, was not a well-known ministry. It had no global platform, no national profile, and no expectation that history would unfold within its walls. Yet on that night, something happened that would draw more than 250,000 visitors over the next several years, shake churches across the United States, and eventually trigger a relocation to Springfield that amplified its influence further still.

The Smithton/Springfield Outpouring, quickly became a living testimony to the truth that God often chooses unexpected places to ignite spiritual fire. Rural farmland, gravel roads, grain silos and modest homes formed the backdrop of a movement that touched pastors, worship leaders, missionaries, families, and entire church networks. What unfolded demonstrated that spiritual hunger, repentance, and renewal are not tied to geography, population size, or denominational prestige. When God draws near, even the smallest congregation in the most overlooked place can become a magnet for the nations.

A moment of personal desperation
The roots of the Smithton Outpouring can be traced to a season of profound personal and pastoral exhaustion. Pastor Steve Gray recounts how he had personally reached a point of spiritual emptiness, frustration, and emotional depletion. Despite years of sincere ministry, he felt dry. He prayed, preached, and laboured faithfully, yet sensed little lasting fruit. The church itself had become weary - faithful but fatigued, committed but spiritually starved. Many members longed for something more than routine Christianity. They wanted the living presence of God.

It was in this state that Steve Gray visited Brownsville Assembly of God in Pensacola, Florida, in early 1996, where a revival had erupted months earlier. While in Brownsville, Gray experienced a powerful touch from the Holy Spirit - an overwhelming sense of cleansing, renewal, and divine presence. He later described it as a deep work of the Holy Spirit that broke through the layers of discouragement that had accumulated over years of ministry. What happened next would become the spark that ignited Smithton.

"God is in the house"

When Steve Gray returned home to Missouri, his congregation immediately noticed something different. On Sunday evening, 24 March 1996, during a worship time, something shifted in the atmosphere of the small sanctuary. The presence of God came powerfully. People began repenting openly, crying out to God, falling to their knees, shaking under great conviction, and worshipping with intense sincerity. A deep, heartfelt cry rose from the congregation - some confessing sin, others surrendering their lives afresh, still others overwhelmed by the love of God.

This was not emotionalism. It was not performance. Those present described it as a weighty, holy presence filling the room - like the tangible glory found in moments throughout Scripture: *"The priests could not stand to minister because of the cloud, for the glory of the Lord filled the house of God"* (2 Chronicles 5:14).

Though the setting was far from Solomon's temple, the spiritual reality felt similar: God had come in power. That night marked the beginning of nightly revival meetings that would continue for years.

The message: Repentance and returning to God

Unlike some revival movements that emphasised miracles, manifestations, or large crowds, the Smithton Outpouring had a distinctive message: repentance, holiness, surrender, and wholehearted devotion to Christ. The preaching was direct, urgent, and conviction-filled. Many who attended said they had never encountered such clear calls to humble themselves before their God.

Visitors described how conviction pierced their hearts while worship played, sometimes before a sermon even began. People wept at the altar for hours. Families were reconciled. Addictions broke. The spiritually numb were awakened. Many who came simply said, *"God met me,"* or *"I found my first love again."*

Repentance was not treated as a moment of shame but as a doorway to joy, freedom, and restoration. As David wrote, *"A broken and contrite heart you, God, will not despise."* (Psalm 51:17). This verse became a lived reality in Smithton as many people encountered forgiveness in a way that transformed them.

Worship that carried revival

Worship became one of the defining marks of the Outpouring. The music was not complex or professionally produced. It was simple, raw, and passionate. Yet those who attended testified that the worship in Smithton carried an anointing unlike anything they had experienced before. The congregation sang with a hunger that could almost be felt in the air.

Some nights, worship lasted for hours. Spontaneous songs rose, with believers crying out, *"Holy Spirit, we need You,"* *"Purify us,"* or *"Draw us near."* Visitors would later say that the worship alone transformed them before a single sermon was preached. Worship leaders learned that revival music is not merely about sound - it is about surrender. When hearts bow before God, songs become vessels of His presence.

A rural revival with an unexpected national pull

Word spread quickly. At first, neighbouring churches visited. Then people from Kansas City, St. Louis, and Oklahoma. Soon, people were driving ten, twelve, or fifteen hours just to attend a single meeting. Then came the buses - church groups arriving weekly from across the Midwest.

As the wave continued, international visitors began arriving: believers from Europe, Asia, Australia, and Africa. Media outlets took notice. Christian networks reported testimonies.

Revival magazines wrote features. The Smithton Outpouring became a recognised term in global revival conversations. What made this extraordinary was the context. Smithton was tiny, rural, and obscure. There was no airport, no hotels, no large facilities. Visitors had to stay in nearby towns or sleep in church basements. Yet they came anyway. Many said they felt *"drawn by the Spirit,"* convinced God had something for them. It was a reminder of a timeless truth: when God moves, people will go anywhere to receive from Him.

Life-changing testimonies

The revival became known for its deep, lasting transformation. Testimonies poured in:

- Pastors restored from burnout
- Marriages healed
- Prodigals returning to Christ
- Drug addicts set free
- Christians revived with fresh passion
- Cold hearts made tender again

Visitors described the meetings using words like *"holy," "weighty," "life-changing,"* and *"awakening."* Many of them left knowing they would never be the same again.

A church overwhelmed by revival

The revival's impact on Smithton Community church was immense. A congregation of under 200 suddenly had thousands arriving monthly. Services were held four or five nights a week, sometimes with additional meetings on weekends. Volunteers worked tirelessly – directing parking, seating guests, serving food, cleaning, praying, and ministering.

The church operated under constant spiritual demand yet also with supernatural strength. They often quoted Isaiah's promise: *"Those who hope in the Lord will renew their strength."* (Isaiah 40:31). It became their daily reality.

The strain of success

As the Outpouring grew, the small town struggled to keep up. Traffic overwhelmed the gravel roads. Local authorities were baffled. Businesses were unprepared. And the church faced logistical pressures that made sustaining the revival in Smithton increasingly difficult. This tension would later compel the church to make a major decision: a relocation that would shape the next phase of the revival.

The Smithton Outpouring did not remain a rural curiosity for long. What began in a town of barely 500 people soon attracted visitors from every corner of the United States and dozens of nations. As the word spread - first through personal testimonies, then through cassette recordings, then through early websites and eventually national Christian media - the flow of people toward the little town in mid-Missouri became almost constant. The revival that erupted in a tiny, obscure church eventually reshaped worship movements, influence national conferences, and help spark spiritual renewal far beyond its local setting.

A pilgrimage to a place no one expected

One of the most surprising features of the Smithton Outpouring was the sheer number of people willing to travel long distances to experience what God was doing. Visitors arrived in caravans of cars, ministry teams came on buses, and international guests arrived by plane, renting cars to drive the remaining miles into rural Missouri. Many had no personal connection to the church - they came out of hunger alone.

The Friday night meetings became particularly renowned. People lined up outside the Smithton Community church hours before the doors opened. The sanctuary was small, seating only a few hundred, and overflow rooms were often packed. Some nights the worship began before all the visitors had even entered the building; once inside, the congregation found a spiritual atmosphere thick with expectancy. Songs were sung with a kind of whole-being abandon, prayers erupted spontaneously, and testimonies brought both tears and shouts.

It was very common for worship to last for more than an hour, sometimes two. The preaching - usually delivered by Pastor Steve Gray - was passionate, direct, and saturated with Scripture. Messages focused on repentance, spiritual hunger, purity of heart, the fear of the Lord, the renewing work of the Spirit, and the necessity of holiness in the Christian life. Listeners often described feeling *"stripped bare,"* as if the Holy Spirit were addressing them personally.

Ministry times were unhurried. People flocked to the altar for prayer, sometimes remaining there well after midnight. It was not unusual for visitors to return home different than they arrived — spiritually awakened, restored in their marriages, freed from addictions, or rekindled in their calling.

A revival of repentance and holiness

While some revival movements in the 1990s became known for outward manifestations of joy and exuberance, Smithton was often described as more intense, more sobering, and more marked by repentance. Testimonies poured forth of people confessing long-hidden sin, reconciling with family members, forgiving old wounds, or surrendering areas of compromise. The conviction of the Holy Spirit was powerful and unmistakable.

It was not unusual for visitors to arrive expecting an emotional experience but instead find themselves overwhelmed by the holiness of God. Tears of repentance were frequent. People confessed their own sins openly, sought counsel, and embraced accountability. The focus was never on the spectacle but on transformation.

This emphasis aligned deeply with biblical patterns of revival. In the Book of Acts, the outpouring of the Spirit produced both signs and repentance. In Nehemiah's day, the rediscovery of Scripture led the people to weep, confess, and renew their covenant with God. In the Great Awakening, Jonathan Edwards described *"deep and lasting impressions upon the heart"* as the surest evidence of genuine revival.

Smithton, in this regard, was firmly within the stream of historic renewal. The outpouring was emotional at times, but it was never merely emotional. It called people to holiness, to obedience, to surrender. It produced lasting fruit.

Worship that carried revival's flame

One of the defining features of the Smithton Outpouring was its worship. The worship team, led by the passionate and gifted musicians within the church, crafted a sound that was raw, fervent, Scripture-rich, and Spirit-infused. Many songs were original to the church, some birthed spontaneously in the meetings. They reflected themes of spiritual battle, surrender, repentance, and longing for God's presence.

The worship services often functioned as extended encounters with God. People sang with uplifted hands, knelt, lay prostrate on the floor, or danced before the Lord. Worship was not a "set" or a "segment" of the meeting - it was the furnace in which hearts were softened and prepared for God's Word.

Visitors frequently remarked that they had never experienced worship so free and so weighty at the same time. There was joy, but there was also reverence. There was exuberance, but also brokenness. Worship was the meeting place between divine holiness and human hunger.

The impact of Smithton's worship spread far beyond Missouri. churches across America adopted songs and styles inspired by the outpouring. Worship leaders returned home transformed, their congregations catching the fire. Conferences invited the Smithton team to lead worship for thousands. In some places, the worship itself became a catalyst for local renewal.

A refuge for weary Pastors and leaders

One of the most significant groups touched by the Smithton Outpouring was pastors and ministry leaders. Many arrived burned out, discouraged, or spiritually dry. They carried wounded hearts from church conflict, crushing expectations, moral failure, or sheer exhaustion.

At Smithton, many found restoration. They encountered the love of God again. They rediscovered joy in ministry. Some wept through entire meetings. Others received prophetic words that confirmed their calling. Still others found the courage to make difficult decisions, return home with renewed vision, or step into new ministry assignments.

This pastoral restoration became one of the most enduring legacies of Smithton. Leaders returned to their churches re-energised, their preaching enlivened, their spiritual lives reignited. Some saw revival break out in their own congregations soon after. For many, Smithton became a spiritual well - a place where they drank deeply and were restored by the Spirit of God.

Opposition, misunderstanding, and the cost of renewal

As with any revival movement, the Smithton Outpouring also faced criticism. Some questioned the manifestations of the Spirit; others debated some theological concerns; some dismissed the movement as just emotionalism or excess. Articles circulated. Debates flared. Local newspapers occasionally covered the story with scepticism. Pastors in nearby towns were divided - some rejoiced, others warned their congregations to avoid the meetings.

Inside the church, the leaders emphasised discernment and the centrality of Scripture. Messages regularly addressed the need for character, accountability, and humility. The leadership did not layer hype over the meetings - they tried to keep revival as grounded as possible, teaching that the Spirit moves where people yield, repent, and pursue holiness.

Persecution also came in more personal forms. Some members lost friends or family support. Ministry leaders faced criticism from denominational overseers. Visitors sometimes encountered resistance when they returned home with testimonies of what they had experienced. Yet the revival endured. Its credibility lay not in dramatic manifestations but in transformed lives: restored marriages, freed addicts, reconciled relationships, renewed Pastors, and churches revived in their mission.

A move that outgrew its location

As the outpouring continued, the small town of Smithton was no longer sustainable for the volume of people attending. Over time, the leadership discerned that the revival needed a new home - one better positioned to receive visitors, train leaders, plant churches, and steward the movement's long-term fruit.

This discernment process eventually led to a monumental decision that would transform the movement and bring about the next chapter of its story: relocating the revival from small-town Smithton to the larger city of Kansas City - specifically Springfield. But that transition, with all its challenges, controversies, blessings, and unexpected outcomes, forms the heart of the next chapter in this amazing revival.

What made the Smithton Outpouring truly remarkable was not only the dramatic transformation of a small town church or even the multitude of visitors who travelled from across the United States. It was the also the unexpected, far-reaching spiritual consequences that followed - consequences that could never have been engineered by human strategy.

Large cities hosting large events often expect influence; you do not expect a town of 532 people in rural Missouri to send shockwaves through the church. And yet this is precisely what happened. The fingerprints of God are most clearly seen when the unlikely becomes undeniable.

A movement that reached the weary

Many who visited Smithton or later the Springfield church spoke of arriving very weary - exhausted pastors, disillusioned leaders, burned-out volunteers, sincere Christians who had lost hope, and individuals who had left church altogether. The mid-to-late 1990s were a spiritually turbulent time. The cultural ground was shifting; many churches were experiencing decline; younger generations were becoming increasingly disengaged. Against this backdrop, the Smithton Outpouring became a place of refreshing for thousands who desperately needed renewal.

It was not unusual for pastors to arrive exhausted, sit quietly in the back of the room, and begin to weep before anyone prayed for them. Stories began to emerge of leaders returning to their congregations with new fire, healed marriages, and restored confidence in the calling of God. Ministry teams who had nearly fractured under pressure found unity in the presence of God. For many, the outpouring did not feel like an event—they described it as a spiritual rescue.

This phenomenon echoed the words of Jesus in Matthew 11:28, *"Come to me, all you who are weary and burdened, and I will give you rest."* It was not merely an invitation; it was a prophecy fulfilled in a small Midwestern town.

Countercultural simplicity

In an era increasingly defined by polished production, strategic programming, and the early seeds of performance-driven church culture, the Smithton Outpouring offered something profoundly countercultural: simplicity. There were no elaborate stage effects, no celebrity personalities, no curated social media presence. This was before livestreamed services, digital branding, or online influence. What people encountered was raw worship, heartfelt hunger, repentance, and the manifest presence of God. One visitor described it like this: *"It wasn't fancy. It wasn't smooth. It was real. And that was enough."*

This simplicity made the movement accessible. It resonated with ordinary believers and leaders who felt overwhelmed by the growing professionalisation of ministry. They returned home reassured that God moves through humble people in humble settings. The message was clear: you do not need to be big to be used by God; you need to be surrendered.

Endurance through controversy

Like every significant revival movement, Smithton/Springfield faced its fair share of criticism. Some questioned the physical manifestations of worship. Others doubted the long-term sustainability of what they saw.

Some accused the church of emotionalism. Some denominational leaders dismissed the movement as a temporary fad or fringe expression. These criticisms were not unique to Smithton; Toronto, Brownsville, and many other renewals faced identical scrutiny.

Yet what stood out was the congregation's endurance. They did not collapse under criticism or retreat into defensiveness. Instead, they leaned deeper into Scripture, emphasising holiness, repentance, integrity, and character formation. They understood that any genuine movement of God must be anchored in the Word. This posture enabled the outpouring to sustain nearly a decade of influence - far longer than most revivals of its kind.

Criticism did provoke important questions, and the church addressed them transparently. Leaders taught on discernment, the fruit of the Spirit, testing prophetic words, and ensuring that worship always exalted Christ rather than manifestations. They made space for correction, and accountability, and pastoral discipleship. This helped the movement avoid some of the pitfalls that weakened other revival streams.

A school of the Spirit

One of the lesser-known yet most influential aspects of the Smithton/Springfield Outpouring was the number of young believers who were shaped, discipled, and equipped there. Many arrived spiritually hungry. Some came broken. Others came with a calling they did not yet understand. What they encountered was not simply emotional excitement but a spiritual school.

Young men and women learned how to pray fervently, how to discern the Spirit's leading, how to serve sacrificially, how to honour Scripture, and how to pursue holiness. They learned spiritual warfare, intercession, and worship at a depth rarely found in ordinary church life. They were baptised, filled with courage, and given opportunities to lead small groups, prayer gatherings, outreach teams, and worship nights.

Years later, many would become pastors, missionaries, worship leaders, youth pastors, evangelists, and church planters. Some serve in rural communities; others serve internationally. Their stories reveal a common thread: Smithton/Springfield was the crucible where God forged their calling.

The move to Springfield: A strategic yielding

When the church eventually relocated to Springfield, Missouri, it was not an abandonment of the outpouring but a continuation of it in a context with a greater capacity for growth. The move allowed a lot more people to attend, provided more space for discipleship, and positioned the church within a city that was easily accessible regionally and nationally. This strategic shift demonstrated great maturity: the leadership was not clinging sentimentally to a geographic location but following the Spirit's leading.

Interestingly, the move also served as a test of authenticity. Some feared that leaving Smithton would dissipate the revival atmosphere. But the move proved that the outpouring was never about a town—it was about the presence of God among a surrendered people. Worship continued with the same intensity. Testimonies continued. Miracles continued. Repentance continued. The fire did not diminish; it expanded.

Long-term fruit: Beyond the headlines

Every revival leaves behind two kinds of fruit: immediate impact and long-term transformation. Immediate impact is emotional, exciting, and often dramatic. Long-term transformation is quieter, deeper, and more enduring. The Smithton/Springfield Outpouring produced both.

Immediate impact included:

- thousands of visitors touched or transformed
- deep repentance among believers
- restored marriages and families
- a surge in intercessory prayer

- healing testimonies
- deliverance from addiction or oppression
- renewed passion for Scripture
- spontaneous evangelism
- reconciled relationships within churches

Long-term impact includes:

- pastors whose ministries were revived
- churches strengthened or replanted
- new churches launched by those touched
  in the outpouring
- international mission involvement
- sustained worship movements
- believers who continued walking in holiness
  decades later
- families who still speak of Smithton as a turning point
- spiritual hunger that continues in Springfield
  and beyond

Many revivals fade once the crowds leave. In contrast, Smithton/Springfield produced a generation of believers whose lives were permanently redirected.

What the global church can learn

The outpouring holds several enduring lessons for the global church:

1. *God often chooses unlikely places.*
   Revival may begin outside the centres of power or influence. God seems to delight in using humble settings to magnify His glory.
2. *Revival thrives in hunger and honesty.*
   Smithton was characterised by repentance, transparency, and spiritual desperation. Revival requires open hearts, not clever strategies.

3. *The Spirit moves where He is welcomed.*
   Smithton/Springfield cultivated space for God's presence: not rushing ministry, not over-controlling gatherings, not resisting manifestations unnecessarily.

4. *Discipleship must anchor revival.*
   Without grounding in Scripture and holiness, revival fire burns out. With discipleship, the fire spreads.

5. *Fruit reveals authenticity.*
   The long-term lives changed by the outpouring speak more loudly than any criticism or controversy.

A legacy of hope

As we look back on the Smithton/Springfield Outpouring, its legacy is not primarily found in dramatic meetings but in changed lives. It is found in Pastors who still preach today with renewed fire. It is found in families reconciled. It is found in missionaries serving in unreached places. It is found in believers whose joy was restored, whose identity in Christ was strengthened, and whose faith was deepened.

Perhaps most importantly, the outpouring stands as a reminder that God sees the hidden places. He sees rural towns. He sees small churches. He sees faithful pastors who labour without recognition. And when He chooses to move, nothing is too small, too remote, or too ordinary for His glory.

Smithton/Springfield shows us that revival is not a relic of past centuries. It is a living possibility - something God can ignite anywhere, at any time, among any people who hunger for Him.

13. SOUTH KOREA'S PRAYER MOUNTAIN LEGACY: A NATION SHAPED BY INTERCESSION

South Korea stands as one of the most remarkable stories of Christian growth in modern history-a nation that transformed from war-torn poverty and spiritual fragmentation in the mid - 20th century into a global centre of evangelism, missions, and intercessory prayer.

Nowhere is this transformation more evident than in the legacy of the nation's prayer mountains - sacred spaces where millions of Christians have sought God with fasting, weeping, repentance, bold intercession, and persistent faith.

To understand what in the world God has been doing in South Korea, one must begin on the mountainsides where believers meet God in the darkness before dawn, where prayers rise like incense, and where revival has been continually nurtured for decades. These mountains are not tourist attractions. They are spiritual furnaces - places where the presence of God has shaped a nation, formed global leaders, and ignited mission movements that have touched the ends of the earth.

A nation forged in suffering, driven to prayer

Korea's modern Christian identity emerged from a crucible of suffering. The early 20th century brought Japanese occupation, cultural suppression, and widespread poverty. The mid-century Korean War brought catastrophic destruction, the division of the peninsula, and deep trauma. Out of these ashes, South Korea experienced what many describe as a national spiritual hunger - a longing for hope, healing, and stability.

Christianity, introduced primarily through missionary work in the late 1800s and early 1900s, resonated deeply with a people seeking deliverance and identity. The words of Jesus offered comfort and hope: *"Come to me, all you who are weary and burdened, and I will give you rest."* (Matthew 11:28). The Christian message spoke to both the suffering of the past and the hope of the future.

Yet what distinguished the Korean church was not simply its adoption of Christianity, but the way it sought God — with tears, travail, and tenacious prayer. Long before Korea became known for mega-churches, its identity was shaped by *intercession*.

The birth of prayer mountains

The concept of retreating to the mountains for prayer is rooted both in Korean spirituality and in Scripture. Mountains have long represented sacred places in Korean culture. They symbolise purity, an escape from many worldly distractions, and encounter with God. Korean Christians naturally developed their own expression of this: dedicated prayer mountains where believers could withdraw for hours or days to seek God.

One of the earliest and most influential was Osanri Choi Jashil Memorial Fasting Prayer Mountain, established in the 1970s by the Yoido Full Gospel church under the leadership of David Yonggi Cho and his mother-in-law, Choi Ja-shil - a woman of immense prayer. The mountain featured small, simple prayer grottos — tiny rooms carved into the hillside where believers could kneel for hours or days in solitude. Inside, nothing more than a thin mattress, a wooden block for a pillow, and a small window looking out into the forest.

There were no luxuries. No distractions. Just Bible, hunger, tears, and the presence of God. Soon other denominations established their own prayer mountains — Presbyterian, Methodist, Baptist, Pentecostal, Holiness. By the 1980s and 1990s, dozens existed across South Korea. But the principle remained the same everywhere: *withdraw, repent, pray, cry out for the nation, and intercede for revival.*

Dawn prayer: A nation that prays before sunrise

If these various prayer mountains were the furnace of Korean Christianity, dawn prayer became its daily rhythm. In churches across the country, believers gather at 4:30 or 5:00 a.m. to cry out to God before work or school. Doors open when it is still dark. Worship begins with soft music and Scripture reading.

Then waves of prayer sweep across the room as believers lift their voices. Dawn prayer is not a novelty. It is a way of life. For many Korean believers, the day cannot begin without meeting God first. This discipline, rooted in the hardship of Korea's past, became the backbone of its revival.

When believers pray before dawn, they embody the psalmist's desire: *"I rise before dawn and cry for help; I have put my hope in your word."* (Psalm 119:147).

Dawn prayer did not remain confined to traditional churches. Even in modern corporate Korea, many Christian workplaces host early-morning prayer meetings. University Christian clubs gather before classes. Christian families pray together before sunrise. The nation rises early to seek God.

The Yoido Full Gospel church: A symbol of Korean revival

Of course, no account of Korean revival is ever complete without mentioning Yoido Full Gospel church in Seoul. This has been the largest Pentecostal church in the world for many years.

The manifestation of revival was not the size itself, but the prayer culture that fuelled it. Founded in 1958 by David Yonggi Cho and Choi Ja-shil, the church grew from just a tent in a poverty-stricken neighbourhood to a congregation of hundreds of thousands.

The key was not programmes or technology. It was *prayer and small groups.*

- *Prayer mountains* where leaders interceded and fasted.
- *Cell groups* led mainly by women who prayed passionately for neighbours, healing, and spiritual needs.
- *Dawn prayer services* every day.
- *Fasting retreats* for breakthroughs.

The church became a symbol - not of numbers, but of *a nation crying out to God.*

A spiritual rhythm that reshaped a nation

As prayer mountains grew and dawn prayer became universal, Korea's Christian revival spread into every part of society. churches multiplied rapidly in the 1970s–1990s. Seminaries, mission agencies, prayer ministries, campus ministries, and healing services flourished. Korea became the world's second-largest sender of missionaries by the early 2000s - remarkable for a nation that was once considered unreached.

This spiritual rhythm - mountains, fasting, dawn prayer, tears, intercession - created a nation shaped by prayer. While other nations saw Christianity decline, Korea saw it explode.

Intercessory burden: Korea prays for the nations

One of the clear and defining marks of Korean Christianity is its intercessory heart for the world. Prayer mountains became global hubs where believers prayed for revival in Africa, missions in the Middle East, peace in North Korea, churches in America and Europe, and salvation for the unreached.

Believers felt responsible for global evangelisation. They prayed with intensity, often with weeping, often for hours. Their intercession created a global spiritual ripple:

- Many mission leaders trace breakthrough moments to Korean intercession.
- Korean missionaries were sent to dangerous places where few others would go.
- Korean worship and prayer-music influenced global prayer movements.

Perseverance through struggle

Korea's Christianity was not born in comfort. It was formed in scarcity, war, political upheaval, and cultural persecution. Therefore, Korean believers learned to persevere - and their prayer life reflects this resilience. Fasting for 40 days is not uncommon. Praying for hours is normal. Crying out loudly, even groaning, is part of the intercessory culture.

Their persistence mirrors Jesus' parable of the persistent widow who *"kept coming"* (Luke 18:1-8), and the early church who *"joined together constantly in prayer"* (Acts 1:14). This persistence became part of the nation's spiritual identity.

The birth of a national identity rooted in prayer

To understand why South Korea became one of the most prayer-saturated nations in the modern church, one must look back to the country's story of suffering, perseverance, and spiritual longing. Few nations in recent history have endured such rapid and catastrophic upheaval: occupation, war, national division, and poverty so deep that South Korea in the 1950s was among the poorest nations on earth. The trauma of the Korean War left millions dead or displaced, families separated, and the nation's psyche carved by grief.

Out of this devastation rose a spiritual cry. Christians - who at that time made up only a small minority - in prayer not merely a discipline but a lifeline, a means of survival, and a pathway to hope. The early Korean church was marked by much hardship, persecution, and adversity. Prayer became the response to every challenge: national crisis, famine, family needs, and spiritual hunger. churches became sanctuaries of intercession, and prayer meetings were often packed, even before dawn.

The famous 1907 Pyongyang Revival, often called the *"Korean Pentecost,"* birthed something quite unique. Its hallmark was not dramatic manifestations but deep repentance, confession of sin, corporate unity, and an insatiable desire to seek God. The revival embedded into the nation's DNA the belief that prayer is the engine room of transformation. *"We must pray,"* became not a suggestion but a conviction. *"We cannot survive without prayer."*

This conviction grew stronger throughout the mid-20th century. As South Korea rebuilt from the ashes of the war, Christians viewed national restoration as inseparable from spiritual renewal. churches multiplied. Believers prayed for protection, for provision, for healing, and for the salvation of neighbours.

Entire congregations gathered to intercede for national repentance, church purity, and spiritual awakening. Dawn prayer became a daily expectation, not merely an occasional commitment. Midnight prayer was common. All-night prayer meetings filled sanctuaries with thousands of believers weeping before God for their families and nation. By the 1960s and 70s, prayer mountains emerged as a uniquely Korean expression of this spiritual hunger.

The rise of Prayer Mountains

What began as small, remote retreats where believers sought solitude soon became sprawling spiritual centres. The most famous, Yoido Prayer Mountain, founded in 1966 by Pastor David Yonggi Cho and the Yoido Full Gospel church, grew into a place where hundreds of thousands would come each year to pray. Carved into the mountainside were hundreds of tiny prayer grottoes - small, cave-like spaces just big enough for one person to kneel, weep, wrestle, and wait on God.

Visitors came from every walk of life: pastors seeking renewal, businessmen asking for wisdom, students preparing for exams, families praying for reconciliation, and believers interceding for the nation's future. Many stayed for a day; others for weeks. Some fasted, others wept, others sang, and others sat in stillness before God.

It became normal to walk through the mountain at dawn or late into the night and hear the sound of intercession echoing off the hillsides: voices crying out "Joo-yo!" ("Lord!"), the rhythmic murmur of thousands praying simultaneously, the sound of worship songs rising from the main sanctuary, and the gentle hum of Scripture recitation from small huts.

Theologically, Korean Christians saw prayer mountains as a fulfilment of verses such as: *"I will lift up my eyes to the mountains... where does my help come from?"* (Psalm 121:1) *"Jesus often withdrew to lonely places and prayed."* (Luke 5:16). To them, prayer mountains were not an innovation but an imitation of the devotional rhythms of Jesus Himself.

Over the decades, dozens of prayer mountains sprang up across the country - Presbyterian, Methodist, Pentecostal, Baptist, independent, charismatic. Each developed its own culture, yet all were marked by intensity, perseverance, and deep reverence for God's presence.

The dawn prayer movement

If prayer mountains were the high places of Korean spirituality, dawn prayer was its daily heartbeat. Known as *saebyeok gido* ("daybreak prayer"), dawn services became an institution. The origins trace back to 1907 when, during the Pyongyang Revival, churches met from 5 a.m. to pray for the Spirit's work.

That practice became embedded in the nation's ecclesial culture. To this day, hundreds of thousands of Korean believers rise before sunrise, walk or drive to church, sing hymns softly in the dim light, and seek God before the day begins. Pastors often preach short messages, followed by extended prayer led collectively by the congregation. A wave of intercession sweeps through the room - everyone praying aloud at the same time, yet with a sense of order and reverence. The practice shapes discipleship profoundly. Koreans begin their day not with busyness but with dependence. Prayer becomes the first voice heard, the first action taken, the first breath of the morning.

Intercession for the nation

Korea's prayer culture is inseparable from its longing for healing - politically, socially, and spiritually. From the earliest days of revival, believers prayed passionately for national repentance and unity. After the Korean War, intercession for reconciliation between North and South Korea became a daily burden. churches regularly hold special gatherings focused specifically on praying for five key issues.

- the salvation of North Korea
- protection for persecuted Christians under the regime
- peace between the two nations
- healing for divided families
- revival in the North when the borders eventually open

Believers view this calling not as a political agenda but as a spiritual mandate. The suffering of the North Korean people weighs heavily on the Korean church. Many prayer mountains have entire rooms dedicated to 24-hour intercession for North Korea.

The Korean church also prays fervently for the government, schools, economy, and military. Verses like *"Seek the peace and prosperity of the city to which I have carried you."* (Jeremiah 29:7) guide many intercessors' prayers.

Corporate unity: A distinguishing feature

Another hallmark of Korean prayer culture is collective unity. While personal devotion matters deeply, much of Korean spirituality is communal. When they pray, they pray together - not silently in rows but aloud, simultaneously, sometimes with tears, sometimes with quiet intensity, but always with a shared yearning for God.

This reflects traditional Korean communal identity, where the wellbeing of the group outweighs the individual. It also mirrors the early church: *"They all joined together constantly in prayer."* (Acts 1:14). Korean believers often describe prayer as something that grows in power when offered together. The unity itself becomes a testimony.

This unity transcends denominations. Presbyterian, Pentecostal, Methodist, Baptist, and independent congregations frequently pray together for national revival. Large prayer gatherings at stadiums or city squares often attract tens of thousands, praying in one voice for spiritual awakening and mission.

A global mission force shaped by prayer

South Korea is now one of the largest missionary-sending nations per capita in the world. This is no accident; it is the fruit of decades of corporate intercession. Missionaries are sent to the Middle East, Africa, Europe, South America, and Central Asia. Many have faced persecution, arrest, or martyrdom.

Yet the sending continues with courage and conviction. Before missionaries depart, entire congregations gather for all-night intercession, laying hands on them, weeping for the nations they will serve, and covering them in prayer. Missionaries often describe Korean prayer as the spiritual fuel that sustains them in difficult contexts.

Prayer mountains also hold missions-focused retreats, where believers fast and pray specifically for unreached people groups. This intercessory infrastructure has contributed significantly to Korea's global mission impact.

A nation shaped by revival rhythms

Korea's transformation from poverty to global significance mirrors its spiritual journey. The revival culture shaped not only the church but the national ethos. Values such as perseverance, discipline, communal responsibility, and resilience have spiritual roots.

Many sociologists note that South Korea's economic rise parallels the rise of its prayer culture. It formed citizens who were tenacious, hopeful, and future-oriented.

But for Christians, the national story is primarily spiritual:

> *Prayer changed a nation.*
> *Revival reshaped an identity.*
> *Intercession became heritage.*

Tensions and challenges

Yet Korea is not without challenges. churches now face:

- rapid secularisation among youth
- prosperity-driven distortions of the gospel
- burnout among pastors
- generational divides in worship practices
- cultural pressure toward busyness that threatens prayer rhythms

Still, many believe these challenges are the very reason Korea needs a renewed commitment to its spiritual foundations. Prayer mountain attendance has fluctuated but remains significant. Dawn services continue. Revival history is remembered. New prayer movements are rising among young adults who recognise the need to rediscover the spiritual wells dug by previous generations.

A legacy still unfolding

South Korea's prayer mountain legacy is not a closed chapter. It continues - quietly, steadily, faithfully. It remains one of the most compelling testimonies to the power of sustained intercession in the modern world.

The story of South Korea's prayer-fuelled revival is now well known within global Christianity, but what is sometimes overlooked is just how deeply this legacy continues to shape the Korean church today. While modern pressures, generational changes, and shifting social landscapes have posed new challenges, the DNA of prayer that defined the birth of the Korean revival still pulses through the body of Christ in Korea.

Prayer mountains still remain active. Early-morning prayer continues. Fasting rhythms endure. And a new generation of Koreans is rediscovering the power of their spiritual heritage - even if in different forms than before.

A next-generation awakening

South Korea today is culturally different from the Korea of the 1970s and 1980s. Young adults face immense academic pressure, high stress, economic insecurity, and a rapidly secularising media environment. church attendance among youth has declined from previous decades.

For many churches, the challenge has been how to pass on the legacy of fervent prayer and spiritual discipline to younger believers who have grown up in a world of smartphones, globalised entertainment, and shifting expectations.

Yet the Holy Spirit has not withdrawn His hand. In countless churches - and small - young Korean Christians are experiencing a rediscovery of prayer. Many tell stories of struggling with depression, addiction, pressure, or just emptiness until they encountered the Holy Spirit in times of worship or personal prayer. Prayer mountains, while less crowded than in past decades, still receive streams of university students and young adults on weekends seeking God's guidance for their future, freedom from fear, or clarity in calling.

Some youth ministries have revived overnight prayer meetings, blending contemporary worship with extended intercession. Others have created digital prayer rhythms - set times for believers to connect online and pray together despite busy schedules. Whether in the sanctuary or online, something is stirring: a fresh hunger for authenticity, for presence, for the power of God.

These young believers do not always pray in the same style or volume as earlier generations, but the longing is unmistakable. They are discovering that prayer is not merely a discipline but a lifeline. In an age of hurried distractions, prayer grounds them. In a culture of performance, prayer gives rest. In an economy of uncertainty, prayer restores hope.

The Korean diaspora: Prayer Mountains across the nations

One of the most remarkable features of Korea's spiritual legacy is how portable it has become. Korean believers living abroad - students, immigrants, missionaries, business professionals - have carried the rhythm of early-morning prayer and the vision of prayer mountains into dozens of nations.

Korean diaspora churches in the United States, Canada, the United Kingdom, Australia, Brazil, Germany, and many other countries often hold weekday morning prayer gatherings at 5 a.m. or 6 a.m., following the model they inherited from the revival era. Some have even built prayer cabins or small retreat centres on the outskirts of cities, functioning as miniature prayer mountains for the congregation and local community.

These Korean diaspora churches have contributed significantly to renewal movements in host nations. In cities such as Los Angeles, Sydney, Toronto, London, and São Paulo, Korean believers have become known for their devotion to prayer, fasting, missions, and Bible study. Their quiet faithfulness has influenced many non-Korean churches around the world, now prompting collaborations, prayer partnerships, and many cross-cultural mission efforts.

When Jesus said, *"My house will be called a house of prayer for all nations."* (Mark 11:17), He described not only Israel's calling but the global calling of His church. Korean believers have embodied that calling in unique ways - wherever they go, a house of prayer emerges.

Prayer and mission: Korea's global impact

Korea's missionary movement is one of the most extraordinary developments in modern church history. By the early 21st century, South Korea became one of the largest missionary-sending nations in the world - remarkable for a country whose church was, a century earlier, barely established. This missionary vision was not powered by strategy alone but by prayer. Korean missionaries often describe receiving their calling during early-morning prayer, all-night prayer, or retreats at prayer mountains. Many went out with little financial backing but great confidence in God's faithfulness. Their stories include miracles of provision, protection, and breakthrough in difficult places.

Korean missionaries have served in Central Asia, the Middle East, Africa, Europe, and the Americas. Some have worked among unreached people groups in remote regions. Others have planted churches in major world cities. Still others have served quietly in humanitarian work, teaching, medical missions, or business as mission. Even in places where missionary presence is restricted due to security concerns, the influence of Korean prayer remains. Some of the world's most challenging mission fields have been shaped by Korean intercessors who spent hours or days in prayer for nations they would never visit.

Challenges facing the modern Korean church

While Korea's prayer heritage remains strong, the church does face real challenges. Secularisation is rising, especially among younger generations. The many demands of modern life make extended prayer gatherings harder for many. The busyness of work and study pressures believers to prioritise productivity over spiritual rhythm. Mega-church structures have sometimes overshadowed small-group intimacy. Political divisions will also occasionally strain church unity.

But these challenges are not signs of decline - they are signs of transition. The Korean church is undergoing a generational shift, and with it a refining of priorities. Many leaders recognise that the church must rediscover the heart of prayer, emphasise discipleship, simplify programmes, and cultivate authenticity rather than performance.

One Pastor recently said, *"We are entering a season of pruning, not ending."* That sentiment echoes Jesus' teaching in John 15:2, *"Every branch that does bear fruit he prunes so that it will be even more fruitful."* Korea's spiritual heritage is not fading - it is being refined for a new season.

A renewal of humility and holiness

One of the hallmarks of the original Korean revival was humility - a deep awareness of sin, a longing for purity, and a passion for holiness. This spirit continues today. In many Korean churches, confession of sins and communal repentance remain integral to prayer gatherings. Believers pray for purity of heart, for the cleansing of the nation, for integrity in government, and for holiness in the church.

This emphasis flows from Scripture: *"Create in me a pure heart, O God, and renew a steadfast spirit within me."* (Psalm 51:10). Korean Christians have long embraced this prayer - not only privately but communally. They gather to repent on behalf of their nation, confessing pride, injustice, division, or spiritual apathy. This humility is part of what God has honoured. A contrite church is a usable church. A repentant church is a revived church.

Prayer mountains and the global future

Will prayer mountains continue to mark Korea's spiritual landscape in the coming decades? Absolutely. But they will evolve. Some may become more technologically integrated. Others may focus on retreat ministry for youth, families, or missionaries. New expressions may emerge - urban prayer towers, digital prayer rooms, multinational prayer networks.
But the essence will remain: a place set apart for seeking God.

The book of Isaiah declares: *"They will bring all your people, from all the nations... to my holy mountain."* (Isaiah 66:20). Korea has lived this promise - prayer mountains drawing people from every tribe, every language, and every nation in a global stream of intercession. In the coming decades, Korea's prayer legacy may well become a key component of a worldwide prayer movement - linking nations, generations, and churches into a unified cry for revival.

A torch passed forward

The final legacy of Korea's prayer movement is the torch it offers the global church. It declares that prayer is not a side ministry but the heart of revival. It shows that intercession can shape a nation, missions can flow from prayer, and a whole generation can be marked by seeking God's face. Korea's gift to the world is not merely numerical church growth - it is a spiritual model:

- Rise early before the day's demands.
- Seek God before seeking comfort.
- Pray as though nations depend on it.
- Worship until the heavens open.
- Intercede for those who do not yet know Him.
- Fast, repent, cry out, persist.
- Believe that God still moves mountains.

This is Korea's torch. And the church worldwide is being invited to take hold of it.

14. REVIVAL IN THE SECULAR WEST

For decades, observers assumed that Europe and North America were drifting irrevocably into full-on post-Christian secularism. churches were ageing, cultural hostility to Christianity was increasing, and younger generations appeared indifferent or even resistant to faith. Analysts spoke of the *"death of Christianity in the West"* and predicted that the church would become a minor cultural curiosity or a relic of a bygone era.

Yet under the surface of this narrative, a different story has been unfolding - quietly, steadily, and now noticeably. Across the Western world, small but significant movements of renewal have been emerging, stirring fresh spiritual hunger in places long considered spiritually dormant.

This chapter explores what God is doing beneath the surface of Western secularism: the rise of prayer movements, university awakenings, church-planting networks, immigrant-led renewal, digital evangelism, and new expressions of discipleship that are resonating deeply with a generation that has grown tired of materialism and empty meaning. Far from dying, the Western church is rediscovering its roots in prayer, mission, and community - and God is breathing life back into dry bones.

A changing landscape: Secular yet searching

The Western world is undeniably secularised. church attendance in Europe and parts of North America has declined sharply in recent decades. Traditional denominations have struggled. The cultural mainstream increasingly views religion with suspicion or indifference.

Yet beneath these trends lies something unexpected: a growing sense of spiritual dissatisfaction. Many who rejected institutional Christianity have not yet rejected spiritual longing. They are searching for transcendence, meaning, identity, and community in a world of fragmentation, digital isolation, and ideological polarisation.

In this climate, the gospel has begun to shine in unlikely places. Surveys indicate increasing numbers of young adults - often labelled "nones"-who, while rejecting organised religion, remain open to exploring spirituality, prayer, and Jesus Himself. In many parts of Europe, belief in God has stopped declining and in some places is rising. In the United States, despite dechurching trends, new church plants and prayer movements have been spreading across cities and universities.

The paradox is striking: while Western culture claims to have moved beyond religion, beneath the surface a quiet revival is stirring - one that is not marked by mass crusades or cultural dominance. It is marked by transformed individuals, renewed communities, and spiritual hunger emerging in surprising places.

University awakenings: A new generation seeking God

One of the most hopeful signs of renewal has emerged in academic spaces - settings which have historically been sceptical of faith. Universities have again become centres of spiritual revival, echoing moments from the First Great Awakening and the Student Volunteer Movement. In recent years, prayer gatherings, worship nights, and spontaneous repentance meetings have broken out on campuses across North America and parts of Europe.

What makes these movements unique is their simplicity. They are student-led, worship-driven, and unprogrammed. No celebrity preachers, no elaborate marketing, no strategy other than lingering in the presence of God. Students gather in auditoriums, chapels, lawns, and dorm rooms - singing, praying, reading Scripture, repenting, and seeking direction for their lives. This hunger is often born out of the very pressures that define university life today: anxiety, identity confusion, loneliness, and ideological fragmentation. Students long for authenticity, community, and truth that can withstand the storms of modern life. When they encounter Jesus—not as a cultural idea but as the living Saviour who speaks peace—they respond with vulnerability and joy.

Some campus ministries report growth not seen in decades. Small groups multiply. Baptisms take place in rivers, fountains, swimming pools, and even bathtubs in student housing. Discipleship groups form organically. Students who once held cynical or hostile attitudes toward Christianity find themselves curious, drawn by the warmth and sincerity they encounter among followers of Jesus.

This pattern echoes a biblical promise: *"In the last days, God says, I will pour out my Spirit on all people."* (Acts 2:17). God is moving again among young people in the West - but this time through quiet persistence, not public spectacle.

The rise of prayer and worship movements

Alongside university awakenings, the West has experienced a remarkable surge in prayer movements. Some operate in dedicated prayer rooms open day and night. Others gather in homes, coffee shops, churches, or online spaces. Worship nights, 24/7 prayer initiatives, fasting chains, and citywide prayer gatherings have flourished in cities once considered spiritually barren. These prayer movements share several distinctive characteristics:

- *They emphasise intimacy with God over emotional hype.*
  The focus is not excitement but encounter — lingering in worship, reading Scripture, and listening to the Spirit.

- *They cross denominational boundaries.*
  Evangelicals, Pentecostals, Anglicans, Baptists, Catholics, and independents gather with a shared longing for revival.

- *They prioritise repentance and holiness.*
  Many gatherings include extended times of confession, reconciliation, and surrender to Christ.

- *They inspire mission.*
  Intercessors often become evangelists. Worship fuelled by prayer becomes compassion fuelled by mission.

In a growing number of cities, many once-declining churches have experienced renewal through prayer-focused leadership.

Prayer meetings that once drew only a handful now attract dozens or hundreds. The Psalms come to life again: *"My soul thirsts for God, for the living God."* (Psalm 42:2).

Immigrant-led renewal: The global church comes to the west

Perhaps one of the most striking — and least recognised — factors in Western renewal is the influence of immigrant and diaspora churches. Congregations from Africa, Latin America, the Middle East, and Asia are breathing spiritual vitality into Western cities.

African prayer vigils fill London church halls through the night. Korean early-morning prayer shapes congregations in Los Angeles, Toronto, Sydney, and Berlin. Brazilian worship plants flourish across Europe. Middle Eastern and Iranian believers gather in homes and small halls, worshipping passionately despite past persecution.

These communities carry spiritual warmth, bold intercession, and missional zeal shaped by suffering, perseverance, and vibrant community life. Their presence is transforming the Western church from the inside.

Some struggling churches have been revitalised by partnering with or welcoming diaspora congregations. Others have adopted prayer rhythms, worship styles, and mission practices birthed in the global South.

This globalisation of faith reveals a profound truth: the centre of Christianity has shifted. Revival in the West is no longer something the West generates; it is something the global church shares.

New forms of church for a new era

Another dimension of Western revival is the emergence of new forms of church. Traditional structures still play a vital role, but many seekers connect more readily with smaller, relational, and mission-oriented communities.

These include:

- *house churches* meeting around tables rather than pulpits
- *missional communities* serving neighbourhoods
- *network churches* linked by relationship rather than buildings
- *creative churches* meeting in cafes, parks, schools, or coworking spaces
- *hybrid churches* integrating in-person and online discipleship

These models are not replacements for historic churches - they are complementary expressions of the one Body. What unites them is simple devotion to Jesus, Scripture, prayer, hospitality, and mission. The book of Acts becomes a lived reality: *"They broke bread in their homes and ate together with glad and sincere hearts."* (Acts 2:46). Many Western believers are rediscovering the beauty of early-church patterns, stripped of formality yet filled with spiritual depth.

Something remarkable is happening beneath the surface of Western society. While headlines often insist that Christianity is declining across Europe and North America, a quieter, less visible story is emerging — one marked by spiritual restlessness, unexpected conversions, renewed hunger for prayer, and sincere openness to the presence of God. The secular West, long assumed to be resistant to spiritual renewal, is exhibiting signs of fresh life. These signs may not always take the form of sweeping national revivals or mass evangelistic campaigns, but they are no less significant. God is stirring hearts in universities, cities, rural churches, digital spaces, prayer rooms, and community ministries across the Western world.

A new kind of search for meaning

Generations shaped by post-Christian assumptions are now asking questions once thought settled. Surveys show that the youngest adults - Gen Z and beyond - are among the most spiritually curious groups in the West. Disillusioned by relentless secularism, distrustful of political institutions, deeply aware of personal struggles, and longing for authenticity, many have begun seeking spiritual grounding.

They are open to discussions of God, eager to pray, and willing to explore Christian community even if they do not initially enter through traditional church doors.

In cities such as London, Dublin, Paris, Toronto, New York, and Los Angeles, pastors report an observable trend: people unaffiliated with any church are showing up in services unannounced, often asking quietly, *"Can someone pray for me?"* Many of them have never read the Bible, have no Christian background, and are stepping into a church building for the first time in their lives. Yet something within them draws them there. In university ministries across Europe and North America, students are forming prayer groups outside of official Christian organisations.

In some cases, these groups begin with no framework at all - just a few students wanting to seek God together. They read the Gospels, ask honest questions, and pray for one another. There is a sense of returning to simplicity: the desire to meet Jesus without religious baggage.

This openness echoes the words of Jesus in Matthew 5:6, *"Blessed are those who hunger and thirst for righteousness, for they will be filled."* Even in cultures where faith is marginalised, hunger creates room for the Spirit to move.

The rise of post-secular spaces

One of the most striking features of renewal in the West is the emergence of "post-secular" spaces. These are environments where faith, after decades of retreat, is allowed once again to influence public life. They do not resemble revival meetings, yet they create unexpected pathways for spiritual awakening.

Consider the recent increase in public discussions about prayer, meaning, and transcendence. We are flooded with Podcasts, documentaries, academic circles, and cultural forums — once dominated by sceptical voices — are now engaging openly with the idea that purely materialistic explanations of life are insufficient.

Secular philosophers, psychologists, and deep thinkers are acknowledging that humans are fundamentally spiritual beings. This shift does not immediately translate into church attendance, but it significantly lowers cultural resistance to the gospel. It opens doors. It softens hearts. It creates an atmosphere where Christian witness becomes more plausible and welcome. And often, when people begin searching for spiritual truth, they encounter the presence of God in ways they did not expect. Jesus said in John 8:32, *"You will know the truth, and the truth will set you free."* In a post-secular landscape, many people are discovering that truth is not merely an idea — it is a Person.

Renewal through worship and creativity

Another dimension of the quiet return of faith is seen in worship movements arising across the West. Over the past two decades, worship has become one of the most powerful tools of renewal - not through concerts or emotional spectacle, but through sincere, Christ-centred gatherings where the presence of God is being experienced in a tangible way. Churches across Europe and North America report that worship nights attract far more visitors now than normal Sunday services. People who would feel uncomfortable in a sermon-focused environment are drawn into worship - sensing peace, feeling God's love, and becoming receptive to the gospel.

Across the United Kingdom, movements like Worship Central and local prayer-and-worship communities in cities such as Belfast, Edinburgh, and Birmingham have helped reintroduce a new generation to the presence of God. In the United States, countless churches, from small rural fellowships to large urban communities, report similar trends: young adults are gathering for prayer and worship out of genuine thirst for God's presence, not religious obligation. Art, creativity, and storytelling have also become real pathways into faith. Christian filmmakers, musicians, writers, and digital creators are reaching audiences who would never attend traditional church. Through beauty, narrative, and imagination, they are awakening spiritual longing - often serving as the first step toward deeper exploration of the Christian faith.

The return of the local church

Despite predictions that institutional religion would fade, many local churches across the West are experiencing renewal precisely because they have embraced authenticity, simplicity, and relational depth. Congregations that focus on community, prayer, Scripture, pastoral care, and meaningful fellowship are seeing lives transformed.

In parts of Scandinavia often viewed as some of the most secular regions in the world - small churches are growing as people rediscover the hope and peace found in the gospel. In Germany and France, immigrant churches are revitalising historically quiet congregations. In the United States, post-pandemic church plants are finding fertile soil as spiritually hungry people look for community that feels genuine and grounded.

What distinguishes these churches is not size, but sincerity. They offer a refuge from the noise and fragmentation of modern life. They preach Christ with clarity. They pray with expectation. They welcome the broken, the doubting, and the searching. In the book of Acts, the early Christians *"devoted themselves to the apostles' teaching and to fellowship, to the breaking of bread and to prayer."* (Acts 2:42). A growing number of Western congregations are rediscovering this model - and finding that God honours it.

Unexpected mission fields in the digital world

The West's return to faith is also happening online. For millions of people, digital spaces are becoming sacred spaces. Thousands of online Bible studies, prayer groups, and digital discipleship communities are forming - many led by pastors or small-church leaders who shepherd global congregations from their living rooms. People who feel intimidated or ashamed to attend a physical church often take their first step toward Jesus through an online conversation, prayer, or sermon. This digital mission field is vast and growing daily. It reaches people in moments of crisis, loneliness, or curiosity - late at night, when anxiety peaks, and when questions feel overwhelming. Christians who faithfully speak the hope of Christ into these spaces often find hearts unexpectedly open.

The apostle Paul wrote, *"I have become all things to all people so that by all possible means I might save some."* (1 Corinthians 9:22). In today's world, *"all possible means"* includes the digital frontier - and the Western church is learning to use it well, as we examined in detail back in chapter 9.

The quiet work of the holy spirit

Perhaps the most encouraging sign in the West is the subtle but unmistakable work of the Holy Spirit in individuals who have no previous connection to Christianity. There are countless stories of people encountering God through dreams, answered prayers, providential conversations, or moments of unexpected clarity.

A woman in London described waking in the night with a strong sense that she needed to find a Bible. An atheist university student in Vancouver shared that he began praying secretly because he felt "drawn to Someone" though he didn't know why. A man in New York City reported that while walking through Central Park, he suddenly felt overwhelming peace that led him to seek God for the first time.

These encounters rarely make headlines, but they are real. They are multiplying. They are signs of God moving beneath the secular surface - gently, persistently, graciously drawing people to Himself. Jesus said, *"No one can come to me unless the Father who sent me draws them."* (John 6:44). Even in the most secular of environments, the Father is drawing people to Himself.

The surprising resurgence of Christian faith across the secular West is not confined to universities, prayer rooms, or new monastic communities. Across Europe and North America, signs of renewal — subtle but unmistakable — are emerging in cities, suburbs, rural towns, digital spaces, and cultural spheres where Christianity had long been dismissed as declining, irrelevant, or culturally obsolete. This part explores these developments, examining how God is at work in unexpected places among very unlikely people, building a new foundation for long-term renewal in a post-Christian age.

The return of sacred curiosity

Another trend across the secular West is the widespread return of curiosity about the transcendent. Sociologists have noted an increase in questions about purpose, meaning, spirituality, and the afterlife among younger generations. While not always expressed in explicitly Christian terms, this curiosity often becomes the first step toward deeper faith.

The pandemic accelerated this process dramatically. As people faced mortality, isolation, and loss, questions once avoided became unavoidable. Many rediscovered prayer.

Others felt drawn to the Scriptures they had ignored since childhood. Some attended church online, free from embarrassment or social pressure. Others found themselves inexplicably awakened to spiritual longing.

In Europe, where institutional religion has often been sidelined, this curiosity has taken various forms:

- renewed interest in pilgrimages (eg. Camino de Santiago),
- classical music concerts featuring sacred works,
- exhibitions of Christian art attracting record crowds,
- packed cathedral services on major feast days,
- new spiritual reading groups in secular cities.

In North America, the shift is equally visible:

- young adults flocking to theology podcasts,
- book sales in Christian spirituality rising,
- record attendance at some Scripture-engagement conferences,
- renewed interest in historic Christian practices (fasting, silence, lectio divina),
- and growing hunger for communities that offer depth rather than entertainment.

People who once dismissed faith as irrelevant are now asking questions. And where questions rise, the Spirit often moves.

The rise of ordinary evangelism

One of the quietest yet most significant developments in the West is the growth of everyday evangelism. Unlike earlier eras marked by large rallies or stadium crusades, today's evangelism often happens over coffee, in workplaces, in neighbourhood parks, or through friendships formed at gyms, book clubs, or parenting groups.

Christians in secular environments are rediscovering the simple power of faithful presence — living visibly as disciples of Jesus, loving their neighbours, and being ready to speak of Christ when the moment comes. The result has been countless conversions across the West — small in number at any single moment, but significant in aggregate. There is a renewed confidence in relational evangelism built on authenticity, integrity, and long-term friendship. People are not responding to marketing - they are responding to lives transformed by grace.

New churches for a new era

In Europe and North America, church planting is flourishing - not only in those megachurch formats but also in neighbourhood fellowships, liturgical plants, micro-churches, and multicultural congregations. This is not the institutional expansion of the past but a grassroots movement shaped by local context.

In Europe, many of the fastest-growing churches are led by immigrants - from Africa, Asia, the Caribbean, Latin America, and Eastern Europe. These congregations often meet in school halls, warehouses, or shared spaces. They are spiritually vibrant, rooted in prayer, and evangelistically bold. Their presence has revitalised Christian witness in cities like London, Paris, Amsterdam, Berlin, and Rome.

In North America, a new generation of pastors is planting churches designed to reach sceptical secular people. These churches emphasise clarity, community, Scriptural preaching, and spiritual formation. Their worship often blends historic liturgy with contemporary expression, appealing to those seeking substance rather than spectacle.

Across the West, new churches are reaching:

- university students
- young professionals
- migrants and refugees
- families with no religious background
- those burned out by institutional religion
- artists and creatives
- digital-native generations

This quiet proliferation of churches demonstrates that the gospel is still powerful in secular places. Jesus' promise remains unshaken: *"I will build my church, and the gates of Hades will not overcome it."* (Matthew 16:18).

Worship renewal and the longing for beauty

Another mark of Western revival is a renewed interest in beauty as a pathway to God. After decades of functional, pragmatic church architecture and minimalist worship, many believers are rediscovering the role of beauty in worship. Cathedrals once empty now host candlelit services with hundreds attending. Choral evensong is experiencing revival in British universities. Composers are writing sacred music that resonates across secular audiences. Christian artists, filmmakers, and writers are bringing biblical themes into mainstream culture with excellence and depth.

Beauty speaks where arguments fail. In an age starving for meaning, beauty awakens longing. It points beyond itself, echoing the psalmist's cry: *"One thing I ask from the Lord... that I may dwell in the house of the Lord all the days of my life, to gaze on the beauty of the Lord."* (Psalm 27:4).

The power of repentance and renewal

In both Europe and North America, pockets of repentance-driven renewal have appeared, often quietly. churches have confessed leadership failures, confronted hidden sin, addressed injustice, and humbly sought restoration. These moments - sometimes painful - have become the soil for genuine renewal.

People are drawn not to perfection but to authenticity, humility, and holiness. This is the kind of renewal the prophets longed for. This is the kind of revival the early church experienced. And it is the kind emerging today across the secular West.

The future of revival in the secular west

While Europe and North America remain culturally complex and spiritually contested, the story is far from one of decline. The kingdom of God is advancing in ways that do not always make headlines but do change lives, churches, neighbourhoods, and nations.

The future of Western revival will likely be:

- local rather than centralised
- relational rather than programmatic
- digital-and-physical rather than either/or
- slow-burn rather than explosive
- built on depth rather than hype
- shaped by prayer rather than strategy

In the midst of secularism, God is not silent. Faith is returning - quietly, steadily, beautifully. The same Spirit who moved in Jerusalem, Antioch, Geneva, London, New York, and Los Angeles continues to move today in cafés, campuses, cathedrals, conference rooms, and living rooms across the West.

The story of revival is not finished. It is being written still - often in whispers, often in hidden spaces, but always with the unmistakable fingerprints of God.

15. SIGNS OF THE FUTURE: GLOBAL TRENDS POINTING TO GOD'S NEXT MOVES

The story of revival is not simply a record of what God has done in the past. It is an unfolding narrative - a living testimony of what God is doing now, and a prophetic invitation to what He is preparing to do next. Every generation of believers stands at the threshold between memory and mission, looking back with gratitude at God's mighty works while looking forward with expectation to His future movements.

Scripture continually frames our faith this way: remembering the Lord's faithfulness while anticipating His next act of redemption. *"Forget the former things; do not dwell on the past. See, I am doing a new thing!"* (Isaiah 43:18–19).

This chapter explores the emerging currents, global patterns, and spiritual tremors that suggest God is already preparing the world for new waves of awakening. Not all of these trends are outwardly religious. Many are cultural, social, or technological — but the discerning believer sees a deeper story beneath the surface.

God often moves in ways that surprise the church and confound the experts. Revival rarely follows predictable lines. Instead, it erupts through unexpected people, places, and environments, reminding us that the Spirit is sovereign, creative, and infinitely wise.

Across continents today, there are unmistakable signs that God is stirring His church, shaking nations, reopening ancient wells of prayer, and drawing people to Himself through crises that reveal the inadequacy of human solutions.

Like the sons of Issachar who *"understood the times and knew what Israel should do."* (1 Chronicles 12:32), the global church is called to read the signs of this moment and prepare for the next chapters of God's redemptive work.

A global hunger for the supernatural

Despite rising secularism in the West, the world is becoming more - not less - spiritually hungry. A surprising trend is emerging across generations, cultures, and continents: the desire to encounter something beyond the material.

In the West, millions of people are rejecting institutional religion while simultaneously pursuing spiritual practices, meditation, supernatural experiences, searching for transcendent meaning. This hunger is not actually a threat to Christianity—it is an unprecedented opportunity. Beneath the confusion is a longing for the presence, power, and truth that only Christ can satisfy.

The explosive growth of the Christian church in the Global South demonstrates that people are drawn not merely to doctrine but to a living encounter with the risen Jesus - through healing, deliverance, prayer, worship, community, and transformed lives. Even in secular nations, stories of dreams, miracles, conversions, and unexpected renewal subtly reveal that the Holy Spirit has not withdrawn from the world. Instead, He is drawing near, preparing hearts for deeper revelation.

The rise of a generation disillusioned with empty ideologies

The younger generation—often characterised as disenchanted, anxious, digitally saturated, and suspicious of institutions—is simultaneously demonstrating a readiness for authentic faith. Many young adults are wrestling with existential questions: What is true? What is meaningful? Why am I here? These questions create a spiritual vacuum into which the gospel can speak with clarity and power.

All around the world, youth-led prayer gatherings, worship movements, student revivals, discipleship groups and campus ministries, are quietly growing in number. They are marked not by entertainment but by hunger - hunger for Scripture, holiness, community, and mission. This is a sign. God often raises up young people at the threshold of major movements: David, Daniel, Esther, Timothy, the early disciples. Jesus Himself called fishermen and teenagers to start a global revolution.

This emerging generation may be more spiritually strategic than it appears. Their dissatisfaction with shallow answers and superficial religion positions them perfectly for a deep encounter with God.

Crisis as a catalyst for awakening

Throughout history, revivals often follow, or accompany crises. Wars, economic collapses, pandemics, political upheaval, or cultural fragmentation create spaces where human strength is exhausted and spiritual longing intensifies. The past decade has seen layers of global instability: a pandemic that shook the world, financial insecurity, mental health crises, polarisation, war, technological disruption, and rapid social change. Though painful, these tremors often prepare nations for spiritual openness.

In many countries today, churches report rising interest in prayer, pastoral care, community life, and spiritual conversation—not despite crisis but *because of it*. The church must recognise these moments not as threats but as divine invitations. Jesus said, *"When these things begin to take place, stand up and lift up your heads."* (Luke 21:28). Crisis can be a womb for revival, not a grave.

The return of the global prayer movement

One of the most important signs pointing to future revival is the global resurgence of prayer. From South Korea's mountains to Europe's prayer rooms, from African night vigils to Latin American fasting movements, from America's college campuses to underground churches across Asia, prayer is rising. Not polite prayer. Not casual prayer. This is urgent, persistent, faith-filled intercession.

Millions are engaging in continuous prayer movements—24/7 prayer rooms, global prayer chains, digital prayer communities, and citywide intercessory gatherings. Prayer is increasingly decentralised, intergenerational, and international. The Spirit is uniting believers across traditions and continents in a shared cry for God to move.

Historically, every major revival -Pentecost, the Moravians, the Great Awakenings, the Welsh Revival, the Azusa Street Revival - was preceded by concentrated prayer. If prayer is rising across the world, then something is coming. God never summons His people to intercession without purpose.

A global church: now decentralised, mobile, and missional

Another unprecedented trend is the reshaping of global Christianity. The centre of gravity has shifted from Europe and North America toward Africa, Asia, and Latin America. These regions now embody the most dynamic, evangelistic, and mission-oriented expressions of the faith. This shift is not a loss - it is a sign of maturity. The church is becoming truly global, multi-ethnic, and decentralised.

This decentralisation mirrors the book of Acts. The early church grew not through physical temples or institutions but through networks of believers empowered by the Spirit. Today, house-church networks in Asia, prayer movements in Africa, worship gatherings in Latin America, and missional communities in the West reflect that same apostolic pattern.

A decentralised church is harder to silence, restrict, or control. It thrives under persecution, multiplies in crisis, and adapts rapidly to cultural change. It is precisely the kind of church that flourishes when God prepares the world for a new move of His Spirit.

Technology becoming a platform for evangelism

As outlined in chapter 9, the digital age - though often criticised for its fragmentation - has also become one of the greatest platforms for the gospel in human history. More Scripture is being read today through phones and digital apps than through printed books. Sermons, testimonies, discipleship resources, worship, theological training, and evangelistic content reach millions instantly. Persecuted believers often rely on encrypted digital resources for teaching and fellowship. Young seekers across continents encounter the gospel online long before entering a physical church building.

Artificial intelligence, translation technology, livestreaming, and global communication networks are enabling gospel access to regions previously unreachable. God is using technology not to replace the church but to multiply its reach.

The rise of holistic discipleship

A final global sign is the growing emphasis on deep discipleship. Many Christian leaders around the world have recognised that shallow faith can never survive cultural pressure. There is a renewed hunger for biblical literacy, spiritual formation, holiness, integrity, community, generosity, justice, mission, and Spirit-empowered living. This is not accidental. It is preparation. When God prepares the world for awakening, He often begins with His people. As the church deepens, strengthens, and humbles itself, it becomes ready for fresh outpouring.

The global re-alignment of Christian influence

One of the most significant trends shaping the future of global Christianity is the dramatic re-alignment of where spiritual influence now resides. For much of the last millennium, the centre of Christian energy, theological reflection, and missionary initiative has been the Western world - Europe first, and later North America. But over the last forty years, and especially in the twenty-first century, influence has steadily shifted southward and eastward.

Christianity is now growing most rapidly in Africa, Asia, Latin America, and parts of the Middle East. These shifts are not merely demographic; they are deeply spiritual and profoundly strategic.

In Africa, new believers gather by the thousands under open skies, praying fervently into the night and planting churches at astonishing rates. In Latin America, charismatic renewal and mission mobilisation have created entire networks of evangelists, prayer movements, and worship ministries that are influencing the global church. In China, the house-church movement - despite pressure - continues to multiply disciples and send missionaries into unreached regions.

And in the Middle East, especially in contexts of persecution, God is drawing people to Christ through dreams, visions, and supernatural encounters.

These regions now carry a weight of spiritual authority recognised across the world. Their testimonies shape global conferences, inspire intercessors, and redirect mission strategies. The missionary traffic of the twenty-first century flows increasingly from the Global South to the rest of the world - including the secular West.

This re-alignment should not be seen as loss for the West, but as gain for the entire Body of Christ. It reflects God's plan that the gospel should grow in every culture, belong to every people, and be strengthened by every community. It also signals something vital: God is preparing His church for a new era of unity, diversity, and Spirit-led collaboration.

A quiet reawakening in the secular west

Despite the dramatic growth elsewhere, the Western world has not been left behind. Contrary to many pessimistic headlines, signs of a quiet and steady reawakening have begun to surface in Europe, North America, Australia, and other historically secularising regions. These stirrings differ in form from the mass revivals of previous centuries, but they are genuine, deep, and remarkably consistent.

In university campuses across the United States and the UK, prayer gatherings have grown quietly but significantly. At times, small groups become hundreds. Some campuses have now experienced long seasons of profound repentance, worship, spontaneous confession, and healing - often led by students with no formal ministry training.

Churches once in decline have begun to regather momentum through prayer and relational evangelism. Many pastors describe a fresh openness to spiritual things among younger generations - an unexpected hunger for meaning, community, and transcendence.

In many parts of Europe now, where church attendance has been historically low for decades, new congregations are springing up: multicultural, vibrant, Scripture-centred, Spirit-filled. Refugee believers from Africa, the Middle East, and Asia are playing a significant role in renewing local European churches. They bring prayer, worship, and evangelistic passion many Europeans have not seen for generations.

Digital evangelism has opened doors that did not exist twenty years ago. People exploring faith secretly online are finding Christian communities digitally, watching powerful testimonies on YouTube, joining prayer groups through encrypted apps, and reading Scripture privately through Bible apps. This quiet spiritual curiosity, often invisible in public surveys, represents a massive mission field emerging right now.

The West may not be experiencing the same revival patterns as the Global South, but seeds of renewal are undeniably being planted - and God often begins His greatest works quietly.

The convergence of prayer movements across nations

One of the clearest signs pointing to God's next moves is the unprecedented global convergence of prayer. Never in history have believers been so interconnected in intercession — continent to continent, language to language, church to church. What happens in one nation now becomes prayer fuel for believers on the other side of the world within hours.

Twenty-four-hour prayer rooms, national days of fasting, digital prayer chains, global livestream gatherings, and inter-church intercession networks have become commonplace. Time-zone prayer cycles ensure that somewhere on earth, every minute of every day, believers are crying out for revival, justice, healing, and the fulfilment of the Great Commission.

This unity in prayer across many nations is not accidental, it is prophetic. When God draws His people into widespread, persistent intercession, it is always the precursor to significant spiritual breakthrough.

Scripture shows this repeatedly: before Pentecost the disciples devoted themselves to prayer (Acts 1:14), before Paul's missionary journeys the church fasted and prayed (Acts 13:2-3), before great deliverances Israel cried out to the Lord (Judges 3:9, Exodus 2:23-25). Prayer is not background noise to revival — it is its engine.

Today's global prayer convergence suggests that God is preparing His church for something unprecedented — something that will require unity, humility, and a posture of listening.

A generation rising with hunger for the Holy Spirit

Another global trend pointing toward God's next moves is the spiritual hunger emerging among younger generations. Despite the stereotypes of Gen Z as secular or apathetic, studies and testimonies show that many young adults across nations are intensely seeking authenticity, purpose, and spiritual reality. They are tired of institutional religion but deeply open to Jesus. They reject hypocrisy but hunger for holiness. They question tradition but long for truth.

Movements of youth-led worship, student evangelism, campus prayer gatherings, and spontaneous repentance have surfaced in pockets around the world. Many young believers show remarkable boldness in sharing their faith online and in personal conversations. They want a Christianity that is lived, not just believed; experienced, not just explained; sacrificial, not comfortable. This hunger aligns with Jesus' blessing: *"Blessed are those who hunger and thirst for righteousness, for they will be filled."* (Matthew 5:6). Older believers often express concern that faith is disappearing among the young. But beneath the surface a remnant is rising - a generation yearning for encounter with God and ready to carry the gospel into the future.

The church strengthened through fire

Wherever persecution increases, another trend emerges: purity, resolve, and devotion deepen. Across regions where Christians face hostility - Asia, the Middle East, Africa, parts of Eastern Europe - the church is refining itself.

Cultural Christianity weakens; committed disciples remain. This is not a loss—it is purification. History repeatedly shows that persecution does not extinguish faith; it strengthens it. God uses adversity to prune the church, revealing genuine belief, solidifying community, and preparing His people for greater impact. The future global church may look smaller in some regions but purer, stronger, more courageous.

This sharpening of devotion among persecuted believers is a sign that God is preparing the global church for greater spiritual power, unity, and witness in the years ahead.

The future is global: A church without borders

The most encouraging sign of all is this: the church's future is global, inter-connected, and multi-ethnic. No single nation or culture will dominate the next move of God. Revival will rise from unexpected places - rural villages, crowded cities, refugee camps, university campuses, prayer rooms, digital spaces. The Spirit is preparing the Body of Christ for a season where every continent contributes, every culture enriches, every nation receives and gives.

This is what John saw in Revelation: *"...there before me was a great multitude that no one could count, from every nation, tribe, people and language..."* (Revelation 7:9). That future vision is becoming present reality. And every sign suggests that God is preparing His global church for a new wave of His presence—bigger than Toronto, deeper than Brownsville, broader than Asbury, more diverse than any previous revival.

As we look toward the coming decades, the global church stands at a remarkable crossroads. The Spirit is moving across nations in ways both familiar and entirely new. The stories in this book— revivals, awakenings, prayer movements, visions, renewed evangelism, unexpected worship cultures—are not isolated events. They form a pattern. They point toward something ahead. They suggest convergence. And they invite every believer to discern the times with biblical wisdom and spiritual sensitivity.

Followers of Jesus throughout history have lived between what God has done and what God is about to do. This tension calls for humility, watchfulness, obedience, and holy expectancy. Jesus said, "Keep watch, because you do not know on what day your Lord will come" (Matthew 24:42). While this refers ultimately to His return, it also speaks to our posture in seasons of divine visitation. When God begins to stir globally, the people of God are called to pay attention. To listen carefully. To stay awake spiritually.

This closing section draws together emerging global trends and considers how they point toward the next great movements of God. These trends are not predictions—they are trajectories. They offer clues. They reflect biblical patterns. And they show how God might be preparing the world for His next works of renewal, awakening, and mission.

A generation returning to prayer and fasting

Around the world, young believers are rediscovering disciplines that previous generations often neglected. All across Europe, Asia, the Americas, and Africa, movements centred around prayer rooms, worship nights, solemn assemblies, and extended fasting are multiplying. In universities, house churches, city hubs, and rural fellowships, prayer has become the heartbeat of a new generation.

This renewed devotion echoes the early church, which *"all joined together constantly in prayer."* (Acts 1:14). It mirrors the instruction of the apostle Paul: *"Pray continually"* (1 Thessalonians 5:17). It reflects the longing of the psalmist: *"My soul yearns for you in the night; in the morning my spirit longs for you."* (Isaiah 26:9).

Whenever God prepares His people for a new move of the Spirit, He first calls them to prayer. Prayer tills the soil of the heart. Prayer awakens spiritual hunger. Prayer aligns the church with God's timing. Around the world today, the frequency and intensity of prayer movements suggest that God is preparing the global church for deeper intimacy and greater power.

The rise of relational discipleship

In every region where the church is rapidly growing—China, Iran, parts of Africa, South Asia, Southeast Asia—the common denominator is decentralised, relational, Scripture-centred discipleship. Faith travels through households, friendships, workplaces, small groups, and prayer partnerships.

This is not a return to old methods—it is a return to biblical methods. *"You know that I have not hesitated to preach anything that would be helpful... teaching you publicly and from house to house."* (Acts 20:20).

As institutional religion declines in many Western nations, smaller spiritual families are emerging. Micro-churches. House gatherings. Student prayer clusters. Workplace fellowships. Simple churches meeting around Scripture and communion. This trend suggests a global reset toward a more flexible and relational form of Christian community—one that can thrive in secular, hostile, or post-Christian environments.

Such decentralised structures allow the church to expand rapidly. They equip ordinary believers to lead. They ensure that spiritual life is not confined to buildings but woven into daily rhythms. This is not the end of the traditional church—but it is an expansion. A widening of the expression of the body of Christ.

A global hunger for holiness and authenticity

Across continents, believers are expressing weariness with superficial faith. They want the real thing—purity of heart, integrity, spiritual power, authentic worship, deep repentance. They want freedom from sin, worldliness, and distraction. They want Jesus Christ. This trend cuts across denominational lines. It is rising in charismatic churches, evangelical congregations, liturgical expressions, and underground networks. It is driven by a generation disillusioned with hypocrisy, scandal, and nominal Christianity. They want the holiness of 1 Peter 1:16, *"Be holy, because I am holy."* They want the integrity of Psalm 51:10: *"Create in me a pure heart, O God."*

Throughout history, holiness movements have preceded revival. Holiness clears space. Holiness restores clarity. Holiness prepares the church to carry greater spiritual responsibility. The resurgence of repentance, holiness, and spiritual consecration across the world, may be one of the clearest signs that God is preparing His people for a new outpouring.

Christianity increasingly moving south and east

One of the defining trends of the 21st century is the demographic transformation of global Christianity. The centre of Christian gravity is no longer in Europe or North America. It is in Africa, Asia, and Latin America. These regions now contain the majority of the world's Christians - and they are the most spiritually vibrant.

This shift suggests that the next major global moves of God may emerge from regions once considered *"mission fields."* For the first time in church history, African, Asian, and Latin American believers are shaping global theology, mission strategy, worship styles, and leadership models.

Their strong emphasis on prayer, spiritual warfare, community, supernatural ministry, and bold witness is influencing Christians worldwide.

God is raising up voices from places long overlooked by Western Christianity. This redistribution of spiritual leadership aligns beautifully with Revelation 7:9: *"a great multitude… from every nation, tribe, people and language."*

A new era of persecution – and courage

Persecution is increasing in many nations. Governments tighten controls. Extremists target believers. Secular elites mock the faith. Legal restrictions deepen. Social pressures intensify. Yet the church is not shrinking – it is getting stronger.

In Scripture, persecution is never the end – it is often the midwife of revival. *"Those who had been scattered preached the word wherever they went."* (Acts 8:4).

Today, the courage of persecuted believers is inspiring global faith. Their resilience is shaping a stronger, more prophetic church.

This trend suggests that God is preparing His people not for ease but for endurance. Not for comfort but for courage. A purified, bold, prayerful, Spirit-filled church is rising from the crucible of suffering.

The return of the supernatural

We are living in a moment where the supernatural elements of Christian faith: dreams, visions, deliverance, prophecy, healing — are increasingly common across continents. What was once a contested fringe is now a global norm in many regions. God is revealing Himself in ways that echo the book of Acts.

"I will pour out my Spirit on all people... your sons and daughters will prophesy, your young men will see visions, your old men will dream dreams." (Acts 2:17). This is not sensationalism - it is a return to biblical Christianity. And as the world becomes more secular, more chaotic, more spiritually hungry, the need for a Spirit-empowered church is greater than ever.

The Gospel crossing every border

One of the most significant signs of God's next moves is the explosion of digital mission — Bible apps, online evangelism, social media outreach, AI discipleship tools, virtual prayer rooms, digital worship gatherings, secure encrypted church networks, and global Christian communication platforms.

Never in history has the gospel been so accessible. Never has Scripture travelled so quickly. Never have nations closed to missionaries been so open digitally. God is using technology to scatter the seed of the Word into every corner of the world.

This trend suggests a future where physical barriers mean little. The gospel now moves at the speed of a click, a message, a shared testimony. Digital mission will not replace the embodied church — but it will amplify it.

Convergence: Streams flowing toward a future outpouring

Perhaps the most compelling sign is not any one trend - but the convergence of all of them:

- global prayer
- decentralised discipleship
- hunger for holiness
- supernatural encounters
- persecution-driven boldness
- rising African, Asian, and Latin American leadership
- digital evangelism
- renewed mission thrust

All these threads are weaving together. All these currents appear to be flowing toward something deeper, wider, and more global. No one knows the timing. No one can script revival. But all the signs suggest that God is stirring His people for a season of extraordinary movement - perhaps unlike anything the world has seen since the 18th-century awakenings or the first-century church itself.

The Spirit is preparing the church. The nations are shaking. The harvest is ripening. The world is longing for hope. And across continents, believers are whispering the same prayer:

"Come, Holy Spirit. Do it again."

EPILOGUE: THE STORY THAT NEVER ENDS

When the last chapter closes and the final page is turned, the story of God's movement in the world does not pause, diminish, or conclude. Revival is never confined to ink and paper, nor contained within the boundaries of a book.

What you have now read across these chapters is not a historical archive and nor is it a museum of spiritual memories. It is a living testimony - a window through which you may glimpse the ongoing activity of a God who refuses to be silent, absent, or distant from His creation.

The question that first framed this journey -*"What in the world is God doing?"* - may have driven us into the stories of nations, movements, and miracles. But now, as the book ends, the same question must turn inward. It must become personal. It must become an invitation. For the God who moves in Toronto, Rio, Lagos, Seoul, and Tehran is the same God who moves in living rooms, workplaces, churches, and neighbourhoods across the world. He is not merely the God of global awakenings. He is the God who draws near to individuals, families, congregations, and communities - one heart at a time.

Throughout this book, the portraits of God's activity have been vast and varied. House churches flourishing under pressure. Muslims encountering Jesus in dreams. Students gathering in worship. Cities transformed by prayer. Nations shaken by repentance. Generations renewed in worship. None of these stories exist in isolation. They are threads woven into a single tapestry - a global pattern of divine pursuit.

But this tapestry is unfinished.

Even now, new stories are forming. New movements are stirring. New believers are stepping into faith. New churches are emerging in unexpected places. New revivals are being birthed in prayer rooms, campuses, kitchens, and hidden corners of the world. Some, you will hear about. Most, you will not.

But the Spirit is always at work, breathing life into dry bones, igniting hope where despair once reigned, calling people to repentance, and revealing Christ in ways that surprise even the most seasoned observers.

This is why the end of this book is not an end at all - it is an invitation to watch, listen, pray, and participate. The same Holy Spirit who moved so powerfully in the accounts you have read is still moving today. And the same Christ who transformed millions across continents continues to call His people to faith, courage, compassion, and obedience.

If the global movements we have explored teach us anything, it is this: God is not finished. He has not withdrawn from the world. He has not abandoned the church. Out God has not surrendered the nations to darkness. His purposes are advancing - often quietly, often unexpectedly, but always decisively.

So, my brother or sister, as you close this book, may your heart remain wide open. May your eyes remain watchful. May your prayers remain expectant. And may your life become part of the unfolding answer to the question with which we began:

What in the world is God doing?

The simple answer:

Much more than we think ... and the story continues.